LEADER'S GUIDE • REPRODUCIBLE PAGES

CONNECT

LIFE & CHRISTIAN FAITH FOR YOUNG TEENS

VOLUME 5

TABLE OF CONT

CONNECT

E • N • T • S

CONNECT Life and Christian Faith for Young Teens
Volume 5 (ISBN 0-687-72139-3

Printed in the United States of America.

This book is printed on recycled, acid-free paper.

Cover Photo by FPG International

97 98 99 00 01 02 03 04 05 06—10 9 8 7 6 5 4 3 2 1

WHAT'S IN A UNIT?

TITLE PAGE

shows the unit title and the session titles; offers a brief purpose statement about that topic.

This Is Not Junk Mail!

may be duplicated and given to parents, guardians, and other interested adults so that they:

- ➤ know what the unit is about and know how they can encourage or participate in conversations about the topic at home.
- ➤ understand the importance of the topic for youth and understand tough questions or realities that youth face about the topic.
- ➤ discover ways to incorporate the topic into family activities.
- ➤ become more familiar with young adolescent developmental issues.

Hallelujah!

offers suggestions for worship in the class setting. Hallelujah! can be duplicated and given to the pastor, choir director, and members of the worship work area in your congregation. Folks can use the worship materials and ideas to help make worship more "youth friendly."

Miscellany

is designed to help teachers who have both middle schoolers and high school youth in the same class. Miscellany gives tips on how to use the unit material with a wide age range, suggestions for special activities and projects, or ideas for intergenerational activities.

Following these unit pages will be session plans for one to three sessions.

WHAT'S IN A SESSION PLAN?

Each session has a specific lesson plan, with options.

Read Me

includes Bible background, material on the teachings of the church, background on the issue or topic, statistical information, developmental background on younger adolescents, and questions youth have about the topic. Read the Read Me page(s) in preparation for every session.

also known as the YouthPage, may be duplicated and given to youth. In most sessions, this includes activities related to one or more of the options in the lesson plan.

There are five connections in each session.
They are:

Initial **CONNECTION**

CONNECT with the Session

CONNECT with the Bible and the Faith Community

CONNECT with Life

Closing **CONNECTION**

YOU ARE IMPORTANT

Younger adolescents need positive relationships with adults. Positive social interaction with adults and peers is extremely important to young adolescents, and you have an opportunity to play an important part in their lives. You will facilitate a group experience from which youth may establish friendships, self-identity, and faith. Youth need someone who will establish appropriate boundaries and allow them to discover who they are becoming, allow them to belong to a caring community, and allow them to explore and establish their beliefs.

That person is **YOU!**

WHO ARE MY YOUTH?

A major research project conducted for The United Methodist Publishing House showed that, in every class, there are basically three kinds of youth.

55% of the youth surveyed are most interested in:
- faith and relationship to God;
- tying the Bible to today's issues;
- learning about the Bible.

30% of the youth surveyed are most interested in:
- belonging;
- a safe place to ask tough questions;
- current events (personal);
- helping others;
- informal talk and music.

14% of the youth surveyed are interested in:
- faith and relationship with God;
- current issues, such as environment, racism, poverty.

One of the keys to an involved class is a variety of activities, with some that appeal to each of these three groups.

HOW DO I SELECT ACTIVITIES FOR MY CLASS?

Each learning activity is designed to achieve a Desired Result. For each Desired Result, choose the option most suited to your class. Try to choose options that will appeal to the youth in your class. If you have more than 45 minutes, you may want to select additional options.

As you "customize" your session, be sure you consider activities that are active and experiential, as well as some that involve discussion and reflection. Be sure to open your class with an activity that gets the attention of the youth. This will help them be receptive to the remainder of the activities. Bringing your class session to an appropriate close is also important. The Closing Connection offers an activity for this. You may also want to use some suggestions from the Hallelujah! page to open or close each session.

IF YOU ARE A SUBSTITUTE LOOK FOR THIS ICON *beside the learning activities in each session. These activities can be done with a minimum of preparation and traditional supplies.*

MINI-WORKSHOP

CONNECT WITH THE PARTICIPANTS

(Allow 15 minutes.)

Before the workshop begins, make copies of "The Seven Developmental Needs of Young Adolescents," from page 9, for the "Connect with Adolescents" section; set up the room, and set out refreshments if you are providing them. Make sure that you have community resource and library lists compiled and available. These will be used in the "Connect with the Community of Faith" section.

SAY:

➤ **Welcome! Thanks for taking time to attend this workshop.**

Today we are going to discover how our families can help nurture and support young adolescents. We will be dealing primarily with young people in the middle school years.

If the workshop participants do not know one another, or if this is the first workshop in the series that you are offering, ask them to introduce themselves to the group and tell the name(s) and age(s) of their young adolescents. Be sure to introduce yourself and identify your role with young adolescents.

When the introductions are completed **SAY:**

➤ **Adolescents are important parts of your families. Sometimes they love being part of your family. At other times they seem to want to have nothing to do with you. Today we are going to explore ways families can be supportive, helpful places for young people.**

(Allow 5 minutes.)

CONNECT WITH OUR OWN FAMILY

Invite the participants to relax, focus inward, and close their eyes if they wish. Ask them to picture their middle schooler(s) in their mind's eye. Then ask them to journey back in their own adolescence when they were the same age as their child. **ASK** the following questions:

➤ **Who made up your immediate family?**

➤ **What was your position in your family? First-born, oldest, youngest, middle, or only child?**

➤ **Who was (were) the authority figure(s) in your family?**

➤ Did you ever challenge their authority? How? Why?

CONNECT WITH ADOLESCENTS

(Allow 5 minutes.)

ASK:

➤ Have any of you ever said, "If I only knew then what I know now...?"

Allow me to suggest that you take a copy of "The Seven Developmental Needs of Young Adolescents" and sit down with your middle schooler to discuss each need. You might ask questions such as,

➤ Do you see this as a need?

➤ How is that need being met in your life?

➤ What could be done to better meet this need?

Be certain to include positive comments regarding ways you, as an adult, might be helpful in meeting these needs. Encourage your middle schooler to think of ways he or she might meet these needs himself or herself.

CONNECT WITH THE COMMUNITY OF FAITH

(Allow 5 minutes.)

NOTE: This will require some preparation ahead of time. Ask your pastor or youth leader to assist you.

At least a couple of weeks before the workshop, gather information regarding ministries your church offers for families. Also gather information regarding the offering of social services for families in your community. Finally, compile a list of books or resources on family life from your church library. Distribute these lists to your group and highlight a few of them.

SAY:

➤ **We are presenting you with a sheet of resources which are available to families in our area. Our pastor(s) and youth leaders want you to know that we are available to support you and your families, too.**

(Allow 20 minutes.)

CONNECT WITH LIFE

SAY:

➤ **Many families report that a successful strategy for building a healthy**

family is holding regular family meetings.

Ahead of time, prepare charts or lists with the bulleted information below. Read each of the items to the group.

A family meeting is a regular, set-aside time for families

1. **to work together to solve problems**
2. **for accountability and responsibility**
3. **for planning**

A family meeting is not

1. **a place where adults tell kids what to do**
2. **a time for blaming**
3. **a time for self-centeredness**

Ideas for making family meetings successful:

-Keep an agenda. Put a sheet of paper on the refrigerator and allow every one to place items on the agenda during the week.

-Hold meetings at the same time each week.

-Begin meetings with Thank You's and end with appreciations or a prayer.

-Always seek to be respectful of one another's thoughts and feelings.

-Allow time for coordinating the family calendar.

-Discuss distribution of chores.

-Discuss money matters.

-Allow time for each person to ask questions or seek input on a problem.

-Set ground rules for behavior. Establish logical consequences for failure to obey the rules.

-Don't expect your family meetings to be happy and blissful. Do expect them to be honest.

-It's likely that the idea of family meetings will meet with initial resis tance. Commit to having family meetings for three months, then evaluate their usefulness after that period.

SAY:

➤ **Please divide into pairs. If your spouse is here, please pair with someone else. Take a few minutes and discuss at least one of the following:**

We already have family meetings and they are...

Some benefits family meetings could bring to my family include...

Some concerns I have about family meetings are...

After allowing about five minutes for this, ask if anyone is willing to share their observations with the larger group.

SAY:

➤ **Let me encourage you to try family meetings for a period of three months. At the end of three months, evaluate them and decide how, or if, you want to continue them.**

CLOSING CONNECTION

(Allow 5 minutes.)

SAY:

➤ **Thank you for coming to this workshop. Let me remind you that our middle schoolers will be studying families in their *Connect* units this quarter. Our Youth Ministries Department wants to be supportive of families and supportive of your young people as they grow to maturity. The journey is not always easy, but it is always necessary.**

Offer a prayer of your own or the following one:

Thank you, God, for families. Thank you for large families and medium families and small families. Thank you for the people who are here today, and for the young people in their families. Most of all, thank you for including us in the most important family of all—the Family of God. Amen.

The Seven Developmental Needs of Young Adolescents

1. Positive social interaction with adults and peers

2. Structure and clear limits

3. Competence and achievement

4. Creative expression

5. Physical activity

6. Meaningful participation in families, schools, and communities

7. Self-definition

(From "The Seven Developmental Needs of Young Adolescents." © 1995 by Search Institute. Reprinted by permission.)

THE BIBLE—THE BIG PICTURE

© JONATHAN A. MEYERS

SESSION 1: THE OLD TESTAMENT—THE BIG PICTURE
SESSION 2: THE GOSPELS—THE BIG PICTURE
SESSION 3: THE NEW TESTAMENT LETTERS —THE BIG PICTURE

Purpose

This unit is designed to give middle school youth the larger context of the entire Bible. This context is related in three basic stories, (1) the story of the Jewish people before Jesus' birth, as recorded in the Old Testament, (2) the story of Jesus and his disciples during Jesus' lifetime, as recorded in the Gospels, and (3) the story of the early church after Jesus' lifetime, as recorded in Acts and Epistles (the rest of the New Testament).

This Is Not Junk Mail!

IT'S IMPORTANT STUFF FROM YOUR TEENAGER'S SUNDAY MORNING LEADER

THE BIBLE GUILT TRIP

I KNOW I SHOULD READ MY BIBLE MORE, BUT..."

If there's one malady more common than the cold, it is probably the Bible guilt trip. It usually sets in about third grade, or whenever a local church gives kids their first Bible. Even though the Bible is a complex, long book filled with lots of foreign and difficult words, adults give these third graders the distinct idea that it would be great for them to read their new Bible (even though most of the adults don't read it much either)! Of course, most third graders really cannot just cruise around in the Scriptures like a scholar, so gradually the pangs of guilt grow with the layers of dust on the unopened gift.

The Bible is the all-time best-selling book, far surpassing any novel ever printed. Yet studies have shown that it is seldom read, basically because it can be difficult to understand. It is about people who lived in another time and place whose customs are often strange to us.

So, what can you do to make the Bible the resource for living it was meant to be?

- *Use sticky notes to mark famous or meaningful passages as you come across them or hear them in worship. (You may even want to begin a family journal of your favorite Scriptures, religious poems and other meaningful articles, or hymns.)*
- *Attend and support Sunday school. This will provide a model to show that we always need to learn more about the Bible.*
- *Instead of reading the Bible front to back (like a novel), begin by reading the Gospel of Mark (it's the shortest story of Jesus) straight through. Then spend some time in Romans, underlining meaningful thoughts. Branch out from there.*
- *Develop the habit of reading a verse or two from Proverbs with your children right after a meal. (Concentrate on the snappy one-liners in the middle of the book—not the longer passages in the first few chapters.) Proverbs was meant as a tool for parents to teach their children wisdom, and it is full of insight.*

DON'T THROW OUT THE YOUTH PAGES!

Why not save the YouthPages from this unit and keep them in your Bible? The first one is a compact summary of the Old Testament in just two pages! The next YouthPage lumps the Gospels into one easy-to-read story, and the last YouthPage tells about the rest of the Bible! In order to understand any part of the Bible, it helps a lot to have an overall understanding of the whole story of the Bible. That way you can see the big picture, and know where the part you are reading fits in. If you sit down and read these three pages in a row, you've been given an overarching look at the entire Bible in less than 10 minutes!

A FEW FAMOUS SCRIPTURES YOU MAY WANT TO MARK

Genesis 1-3 (Creation & Garden of Eden)

Genesis 6-9 (Noah & the Ark)

Isaiah 9:2-9 (People who walked in darness have seen a great light.)

Isaiah 40:27-31 ("wings like eagles")

Job (explores when bad things happen to good people)

Psalms 8, 23, 27, 46, 51, 100, 103, 121, 139, 150

Jonah

Matthew 1-2; Luke 2:1-20 (Christmas stories)

Matthew 5-7 (Jesus' Sermon on the Mount)

All four Gospels, Matthew, Mark, Luke, and John, are full of famous Scriptures!

Easter stories (at the end of Matthew, Mark, Luke, and John)

Acts 2 (Pentecost Story the coming of the Holy Spirit)

Romans 5 (How we are put right with God)

Romans 8:31-39 ("[Nothing] will be able to separate us from the love of God."

1 Corinthians 13 (love chapter)

Ephesians 6:10-20 ("Put on the whole armor of God.")

Ephesians 4:1-16 (the unity of the body of Christ)

James (practical applications of our Christian faith)

1 John 4:7-21 (God is love.)

Revelation 3:20 ("Listen! I am standing at the door, knocking;")

Revelation 21:1-8 (Jesus the Alpha and Omega, beginning and end)

Hallelujah!

IDEAS FOR PEOPLE WHO PLAN WORSHIP

How about a joke to lighten things up?

A woman came into a religious bookstore to buy a Bible for her deceased aunt. She said, "My aunt was such a faithful church member, I'd like to place a Bible in her hands before we bury her."

"I'm sorry to hear about your aunt," said the clerk. "But I'm sure we can find just what you're looking for." Unfortunately, the customer rejected one Bible after another.

"That one's too big." "That one's too expensive." "That one's the wrong color. I wanted a white leather one." Finally, the clerk was down to one last Bible. It was small, white leather, and not too expensive. To her relief, the customer said, "I'll buy it!"

However, at the counter the customer opened the Bible, snapped it shut, and promptly handed it back. "I can't take this one after all," she announced. "Why not?" queried the exasperated shop owner. "The print is way too small," she replied.

Usually we only think of someone reading Scripture in church. Try these other ways to incorporate Scripture in church:

Use a portion of a psalm (or all of it) for a responsive reading.

Use directed silent reading. Have the congregation read a particular passage silently. It might be effective to "set up" the moments of silent reading with a question, so they are reading in order to find a specific answer or message.

Use the power of contrast. Before reading or telling about a Scripture containing good news, say a few words about what it would mean if the opposite were true. Example: Before reading Psalm 23, point out that some people feel like they are on their own in the world, with no God to watch out for them and care for their needs.

Make a banner with a Scripture on it and display it.

Have youth or adults act out a biblical story. With less preparation, they could each simply read the words of one of the characters (including narrator).

Include a Scripture in your bulletin for meditation before worship.

Have youth make artwork, or an audio or video tape to illustrate a Scripture.

Before reading a Scripture, say a few words that summarize what will happen in the text, or make people listen for what will happen next, or set the historical context, or otherwise give listeners a specific reason to listen, or explain the special appreciation of the significance of the text.

If a hymn is based upon or includes Scripture, read or explain the Scripture before singing the hymn. Music is one of the most powerful ways to get a message across.

Miscellany

IDEAS FOR TEACHERS

If your class is a combined class of youth in grades 6-12, it may be helpful to know some of the differences you may encounter.

When studying the Bible with youth of various ages:

- A sixth grader is more likely to focus on the literal level of the story, such as "What was the man's name who was swallowed by a whale?" A senior in high school is more likely to be able to grasp abstract concepts which lie behind a story, such as what does the Jonah story mean about our calling in life? whether or not we should "run" from God, and so forth.
- The developmental differences illustrated above are a healthy process. Some people are stuck on the literal level all their life and never do learn to apply the ideas behind the stories to their life.
- Encourage youth to grow in this direction by asking questions about the truth, symbolism, and meaning behind the stories they have learned as children, but also accept the fact that the Bible is meaningful on both levels, and God is at work through both stages of mental/spiritual development.

AN IDEA FOR YOUTH OF ANY AGE

Keep a Bible journal throughout this unit, or begin one now, which youth might keep indefinitely. Think of this as a resource they might even take with them to college someday. Use a small, bound notebook, or a three-ring binder for the journal. Have youth collect Scriptures that mean something special to them, and perhaps add notes to them such as "something to read when you feel down." The famous Scripture references on the teacher pages for each session might serve as a good beginning point for this project.

The Apostle's Creed, Traditional Version

I believe in God the Father Almighty,
maker of heaven and earth;

And in Jesus Christ his only son our Lord:
who was conceived by the Holy Spirit,
born of the Virgin Mary,
suffered under Pontias Pilate,
was crucified, dead, and buried;
the third day he rose from the dead;
he ascended into heaven,
and sitteth at the right hand of God the Father Almighty;
from thence he shall come to judge the quick and the dead.

I believe in the Holy Spirit,
the holy catholic church,
the communion of saints,
the forgiveness of sins,
the resurrection of the body,
and the life everlasting. Amen.

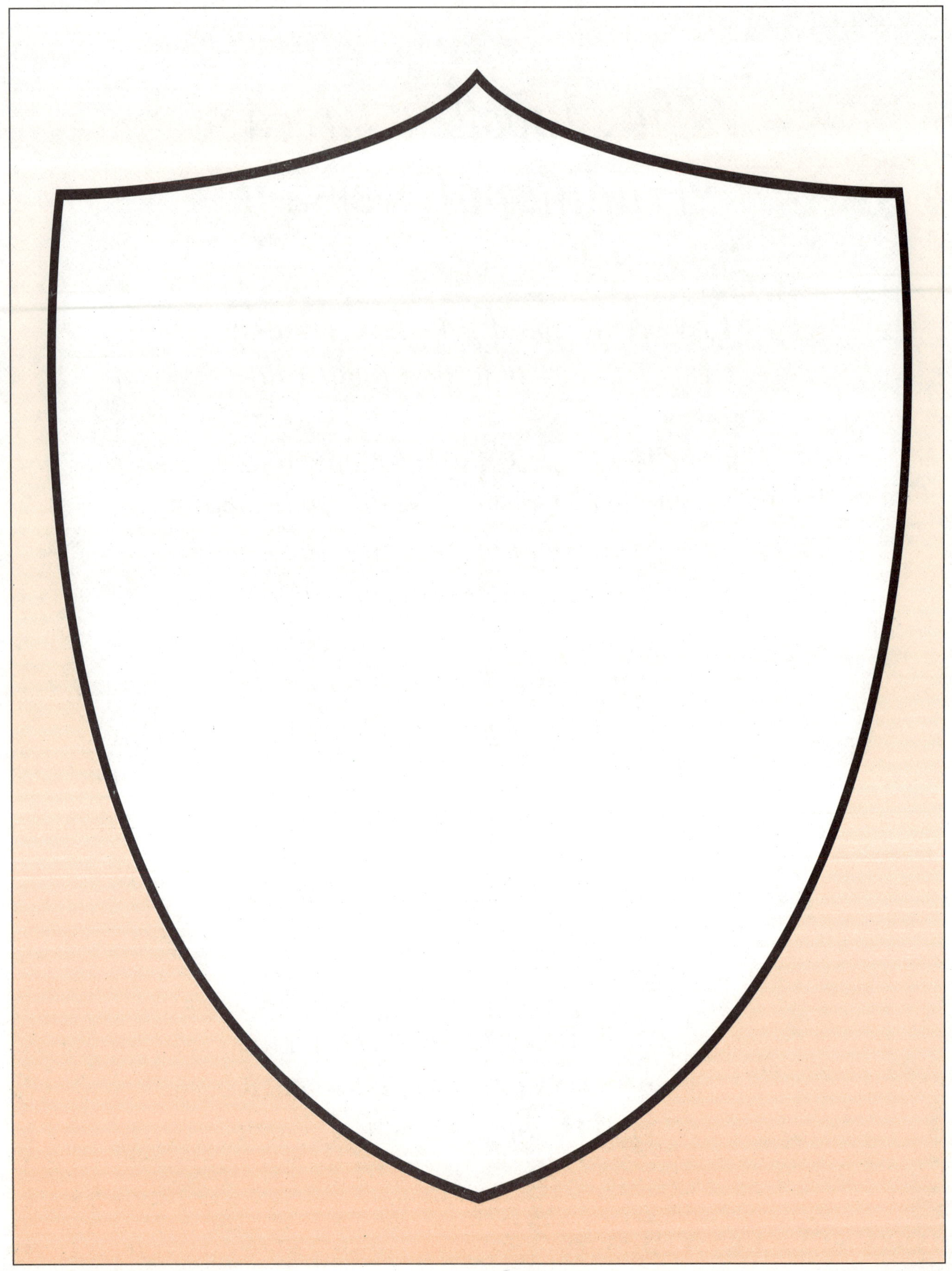

SESSION 1:

THE OLD TESTAMENT—THE BIG PICTURE

FOCUS

The Old Testament is a book filled with many kinds of writing, but each kind is of value to us as we seek to understand God and do God's will.

SCRIPTURE

Ezekiel 1:28b-3:3

HERE'S THE PLAN | **DO IT YOUR WAY**

OPTIONS	TIME (minutes)	PREPARATION	SUPPLIES
INITIAL CONNECTION			
A Honey Scrolls	10	prepare food and clean-up supplies before class	pita or other flat bread, peanut butter, honey, utensils
B Will the Real Scripture Please Stand Up?	12	get Bibles, paper, pencils	Bibles, paper, pencils
CONNECT WITH THE SESSION			
A Class Poem	10	prepare poem, story and prayer pages	Bibles, paper, pencils
B Different Ways to Say the Same Thing	10	look up Proverbs 22:17-24:22	Bibles, paper, pencils
CONNECT WITH THE BIBLE AND THE FAITH COMMUNITY			
A Bible Timeline	15	prepare index cards; make copies and study YouthPage	index cards, YouthPage,
B Two-page Old Testament Basketball Game	15	make copies of, and study, YouthPage	YouthPage, newsprint, markers
CONNECT WITH LIFE			
A Newspaper Spokespeople	10	bring newspapers to class	newspapers, Bibles, newsprint, markers
B Favorite Scripture	10	interview or invite church members to explain their favorite Scriptures	Bibles
CLOSING CONNECTIONS			
Read Isaiah 55:1-11	2		Bible

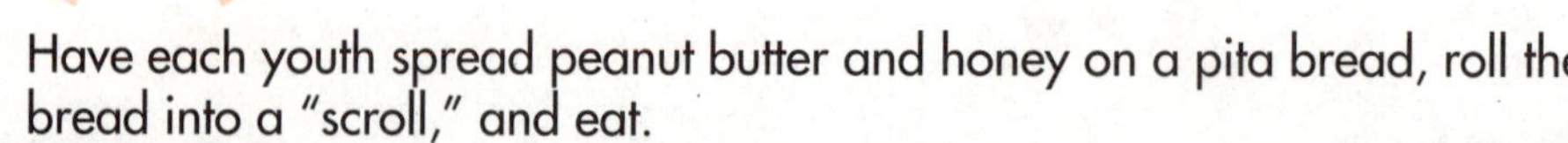

INITIAL CONNECTION

Desired Result:
To provide a group ice-breaker and introduction to the lesson.
(Choose Option A or B.)

HONEY SCROLLS

A

pita bread or other flat bread, peanut butter, honey, utensils
(Allow 10 minutes.)

Have each youth spread peanut butter and honey on a pita bread, roll the bread into a "scroll," and eat.

SAY:

➤ **Ezekiel had a vision in which God gave him a scroll of the Bible to eat. He ate it and said it tasted as sweet as honey. Sometimes we talk about words as if they are something we eat. For instance, we say that "she took in every word," or "that compliment was easy to swallow." We refer to some talk as "sweet" or "sugar-coated," or on the other hand, "poisonous."**

As a class, name a few compliments or Scriptures that seem as "sweet as honey."

WILL THE REAL SCRIPTURE PLEASE STAND UP?

B

Bibles, paper, pens
(Allow 12 minutes.)

Divide the youth into two teams. Each team should create four entries for the contest. Two entries should come directly from the Old Testament, and each entry should be exactly one verse long. It is OK to look for obscure, strange verses to attempt to trick the other side. The other two entries should be made up, but sound as much like a genuine Scripture as possible. For example, "At God's command, Moses and all of the animals got into the ark." (It was Noah's Ark, not Moses'.)

When the teams have their entries ready, ask each team to choose four "contestants." One team's contestants sit in chairs in a row, in game show style. Have each contestant read one of their team's entries aloud to the other team. Give the other team two Bibles. They must decide, as a group, which two are genuine Scriptures, and lay the Bibles on the laps of the two contestants they think are reading genuine Scripture verses. At that point, ask, "Will the real Scriptures please stand up?" Note how accurate the guesses were. If you are familiar with the context, reinforce the Scriptures selected by briefly telling the story or something about the context. Then swap sides and let each team play the other role.

CONNECT WITH THE SESSION

CLASS POEM

Desired Result:
To understand that the Bible contains a variety of types of literature to express faith.
(Choose Option A or B.)

Bibles, paper, pencils
(*Allow 10 minutes.*)

Write a poem, story, and a prayer about Noah's Ark as a class.

On top of one sheet of paper, write "Noah's Poem." On top of a second sheet, write "Noah's Story." On top of a third, write "Noah's Prayer." (If you have a large class, create and distribute enough additional copies of these pages so that youth will always have one available to look at or work on.)

Have youth sit around a table. Give each sheet of paper to a youth, but spread them out evenly around the circle so youth will either have a sheet to work on or be sitting next to someone who has one. Encourage youth who do not have a page to consult with someone who does about what they should write.

SAY:

➤ **In the Bible, there are historical records, stories, poems, prayers, parables, laws, wise sayings (kind of like bumper stickers), prophecies, and many other types of writing. All of these types of writing serve the purpose of expressing the faith of the people. Sometimes, the same event is expressed in more than one way. For example, the story of God parting the waters during the Exodus is told as a story, captured in poetry, and included in prayers. When we read the Bible, it is interesting to keep in mind what kind of writing we are reading.**

Pass the papers around the circle clockwise. Instruct the youth to write a sentence on each page as it comes to him or her, adding to the poem or prayer or story that is already on the page. Encourage them to be creative. Humor is great, and the story does not need to end like the version in the Bible. (However, you might want to compare their version to the biblical one in Genesis 6-9 if time allows.)

INVENT DIFFERENT WAYS TO SAY THE SAME THING

Bibles, paper, pencils
(*Allow 10 minutes.*)

SAY:

➤ Proverbs is one of the most fun books in the Old Testament to read because the proverbs are so short, and because they were originally written to teach youth how to live a good, successful, and faithful life. A proverb is a lot like a bumper sticker. It is a short saying that helps teach us the difference between being wise and being foolish. Sometimes Jesus made a point in his teachings by quoting or making up a proverb. (For example, Matthew 7:7-8, Matthew 7:12, Matthew 18:2-4, Matthew 20:16, Matthew 22:21.)

Ask the students to rewrite in their own words one of the thirty wise sayings found in Proverbs 22:17-24:22. They may choose to make up a story which makes the same point, compose a poem, or write a prayer asking God for the wisdom to do what the proverb states. Let volunteers read their creations for the class, and post them around the room.

SAY:

➤ **There are many kinds of writing in the Bible, including historical records, stories, poems, prayers, parables, laws, wise sayings, and prophecies. All of these types of writing serve the purpose of expressing the faith of the people. When we read the Bible, it is helpful to keep in mind what kind of writing we are reading.**

CONNECT WITH THE BIBLE AND THE FAITH COMMUNITY

Desired Result:
To see the overall Old Testament as a single story, and to see the relationship of the various books to that story.
(Choose Option A or B.)

A BIBLE TIMELINE

prepared index cards, Youth Page
(Allow 15 minutes.)

Before the session, write the names of the major characters of the Old Testament (see the Read Me page) on separate index cards. On the back of each card, write the description, which is in parenthesis. Pass the cards out to the students. Tell them they may refer to the YouthPage, and ask them to arrange the cards in chronological order (character's name facing up). If time allows, ask for a volunteer to briefly retell the story of the Old Testament using the front and back of the cards as a guide.

B TWO-PAGE OLD TESTAMENT BASKETBALL GAME

YouthPage, newsprint, markers
(Allow 15 minutes.)

Before class begins, copy the words below (but not the suggested answers found in the parenthesis) on the newsprint.

First, tell the class that you want to compare the history of Israel to a basketball game. With that in mind, give everyone a few minutes to silently read the newsprint. Then ask the class to help you compare the basketball words on the newsprint with the Israelites' story. Write their answers on the newsprint. Ask them to explain their comparisons to help the class understand the overall picture of the Old Testament.

Referee (God, perhaps the prophets)
Rule book (Ten Commandments)
Team members (Israelites)
Team founding family (Abraham, Isaac & Jacob)
Coach (Moses, Joshua, other judges and kings)
Opponents (Pharaoh & the Egyptians, Babylonians, Assyrians)
Game (time in the Promised Land)
Practice (time in the desert)
Overtime buzzer-beater shot (Ezra/Nehemiah's effort to rebuild the destroyed kingdom)
Trophy (many descendants, life in the Promised Land)
Reporters and news media (those who wrote the various writings)
Cheerleaders (priests, or perhaps the kings, prophets, or other leaders)
Cheers (Psalms)

CONNECT WITH LIFE

NEWSPAPER SPOKESPEOPLE

A

Desired Result:
To begin to apply the Bible to daily life. **(Choose Option A or B.)**

newspapers, Bibles, newsprint, markers
(Allow 10 minutes.)

Provide a pile of newspapers for the youth to look through. Ask them to search the newspaper articles for spokespeople. When they find one, ask them to mark the name and position, who they speak for, and what message they bring. Ask them to compare some of their spokespersons with Ezekiel 1:28b-3:3.

SAY:

➤ **Like all the prophets, Ezekiel was a spokesperson for God. But you don't have to be a prophet to be a spokesperson for God. All you have to do is want to share God's message with other people. We can hear and understand God's message from the Bible; and, as Ezekiel found, it is as sweet as honey! That means it is good news for us and for others.**

ASK:

➤ **What are some situations at school or at other places where you might have the possibility of speaking God's message to others (maybe a word of friendship and hope to someone who just got dumped by a boyfriend or girlfriend)? What effect do you think it might have if you did? Did Ezekiel seem to feel comfortable speaking for God? How comfortable do you feel about speaking God's message to others?**

FAVORITE SCRIPTURE

B

guest speaker, Bibles
(***Allow 10 minutes.***)

In advance, ask a member of your church to find their favorite Scripture, and talk about it with your class. Encourage her or him to explain how this Scripture has made a difference in his or her life, and how it might make a difference to the youth.

CLOSING CONNECTIONS

ISAIAH 55:1-11

Desired Result:
To be thankful to God for speaking to us through the Scriptures.

Bibles
(***Allow 2 minutes.***)

Ask the class to silently read Isaiah 55:1-11. Ask them to underline the sentence in this Scripture passage that summarizes their understanding of today's lesson. If time allows, invite volunteers to talk about the sentence they chose and why.

NOTE: Before you dismiss the class, ask youth to bring in sports cards, featuring heroes and superstars from their favorite sports. These will be used in next week's session.

Read Me

THIS IS WHAT YOU NEED TO KNOW ABOUT THE TOPIC.

DID EZEKIEL REALLY EAT A SCROLL?

Hopefully not! Scrolls were made of sheepskin leather, and would be more likely to give him a stomach ache than taste as sweet as honey! Remind youth that Ezekiel 1:28b-3:3 was a vision! In the Bible, as in real life, it is important to distinguish dreams or visions from reality. However, in the Bible dreams and visions are thought to be one way that God spoke to people. (A New Testament example is when God told Joseph in a dream when it was safe to bring Jesus back to Nazareth. See Matthew 2:13-20.) Like dreams, visions often contain powerful or exaggerated or otherworldly imagery. In Ezekiel's case, this vision explains his call to be a prophet, which means the experience during which he felt his mission in life was to be a spokesperson for God. By taking in God's words, he was then able to speak them to others.

Thus, this passage contains a great rationale for us to study the Scriptures. When we "consume" the Bible, it helps us understand God's will (much like receiving a vision reveals God's will). When we read the Bible, it is "sweeter than honey." It is a good way to spend time and get our priorities straight, and it gives us strength to do God's will for others.

SOME OF THE MAJOR OLD TESTAMENT CHARACTERS IN ORDER OF APPEARANCE!

God (See Genesis 1:1—before creation, God was already there!)

Adam & Eve (first humans)

Noah (built an ark)

Abraham (first received God's promise of many descendants and promised land)

Isaac (Abraham's son)

Jacob (Isaac's son)

Joseph (one of Jacob's twelve sons; star of "Joseph & the Amazing Technicolor Dreamcoat")

Moses (led the Jewish people out of Egypt and to the Promised Land)

Ten Commandments (ten laws given by God to the Israelites in the wilderness)

Joshua (helped the Jewish people conquer the promised land)

Samson (a strong man when his hair was long; one of the judges of Israel)

Samuel (the last judge of Israel)

Saul (the first king of Israel)

David (thought to be the greatest king of Israel)

"FAMOUS" OLD TESTAMENT SCRIPTURES YOU MAY WANT TO LOOK UP

Solomon (last king before Israel split into north and south kingdoms)

Babylonians (Israel's enemy who conquered them)

Ezra/Nehemiah (they led the Israelites as they rebuilt their kingdom)

A FEW "FAMOUS" OLD TESTAMENT SCRIPTURES YOU MAY WANT TO LOOK UP IN CLASS OR PASS ON TO YOUR CLASS IN WRITTEN FORM

Genesis 1-3 (Creation & Garden of Eden)

Genesis 6-9 (Noah & the Ark)

Exodus 1-15 (Birth of Moses, the Exodus)

Exodus 20:1-17 (The Ten Commandments)

Isaiah 9:2-9 ("People who walked in darkness have seen a great light;")

Isaiah 40: 27-31 ("on eagle's wings");

Isaiah 52:13-53:12 (suffering servant)

Job (explores when bad things happen to good people)

Psalms 8, 23, 27, 46, 51, 100, 103, 121, 139, 150

Proverbs (whole book!)

Ecclesiastes 3 (A time for everything)

Jonah 1-4 (a man, a big fish, and a worm)

THE BIG PICTURE
THE TWO-PAGE VERSION OF THE ENTIRE OLD TESTAMENT

SESSION 1: THE OLD TESTMENT—THE BIG PICTURE

The Old Testament can be divided between history, prophets, and writings. First, it helps to know a little bit about the HISTORY behind it. By the way, all of the books in the Old Testament are mentioned somewhere below. Can you find all of them?

The first eleven chapters of Genesis contain the famous stories of creation, Noah's Ark, and others. They tell us that God made our world a good place, but humans have the choice of being good or bad. Ever since Adam and Eve got thrown out of the Garden of Eden for eating the forbidden fruit, humans have had to wrestle with that choice and its consequences. In a way, that's what the whole Old Testament is about—obey and be rewarded; or disobey and get punished. (Does this sound a little like parents?)

In Genesis 12, God made a special promise to Abraham that 1) he would have a lot of descendants, and 2) they would get to live in a "promised land." So Abraham, his son, Isaac, and Isaac's son, Jacob, (who had twelve sons, including Joseph and his amazing technicolor dreamcoat) became known as the fathers of the Jews. In return for this great promise, God asked the Jewish people to keep God #1 in their life. Often they did. Sometimes they didn't. Well, let's move on.

Exodus tells how the Jewish people escaped under the leadership of Moses, through the parted waters, from slavery in Egypt. There are snakes and blood and plagues and mean 'ole Pharaoh in there somewhere, but never mind that now. Moses is still leading the sometimes committed, but usually grumpy people in the books of Leviticus, Numbers, and Deuteronomy. As the story continues, the Jews wander in the desert, get the Ten Commandments on a mountain, and grow in numbers (like God promised...remember?). They learn how to be faithful to God, and basically they get their act together.

Finally, under the military leadership of Joshua, they conquer the promised land (called "Israel," which is good because they are called the "Israelites"). For a while, things were going great; lots of Abraham's descendants living in God's Promised Land.

THE BIG PICTURE
THE TWO-PAGE VERSION OF THE ENTIRE OLD TESTAMENT

Judges, Samuel, Kings, and Chronicles continue the story in the Promised Land. At first they were ruled by Judges (like Samson, who really hated to get his hair cut...Judges 16:17 tells why), because they figured their only "king" was God. But later, they wanted a king like other countries had. So Samuel was the last judge, and Saul became their first king.

He wasn't too faithful to God, so he was replaced by David. David was so great that later the Jewish people figured the Messiah would have to be one of his direct descendants. (By the way, David wrote lots of the Psalms and was a good dancer too.)

Solomon took over after David, but unfortunately his sons couldn't hold the kingdom together and it split north and south. Eventually the north part was conquered by the mean old Assyrians, and later the Babylonians just clobbered the south. That would be the end of the story, and of God's promise, except that later the heroes Ezra and Nehemiah helped the people rebuild the kingdom. Therefore, God's promise lived on; and that's the "happily ever after" ending of the Old Testament story!

Meanwhile, the PROPHETS spoke, and their sermons are written in the Bible. They were a lot like preachers. They told people what God wanted them to do. Sometimes people listened to them, but sometimes they had to learn the hard way. Isaiah, Jeremiah, and Ezekiel are called "major prophets" because their books are long. The other prophets are Hosea, Joel, Amos, Obadiah, Micah, Nahum, Habakkuk, Zephaniah, Haggai, Zechariah, and Malachi.

The WRITINGS are a variety of books which are not history or prophets either. For example, Psalms are poetic words and songs the Jews used in church. Proverbs are like bumper stickers, and if you read them you gain a lot of wisdom. Lamentations (a "lament" is like crying) was written by the prophet Jeremiah after the Jewish people were thrown out of the Promised Land. The writer of Ecclesiastes wonders aloud about the meaning of life. The book of Job explores the problem of bad things happening to good people. Ruth, Esther, and Daniel (yes, with the Lion's den and the guys in the fiery furnace) are also special, wonderful writings. And remember Jonah? That one is a "Whale of a Tale!" (But there's a hungry worm in Jonah too; do you know what it ate?)

Well, that's about it. History, prophets, and writings. Then you come to the New Testament, but we'll leave that for another day!

SESSION 2:

THE GOSPELS—THE BIG PICTURE

FOCUS

To gain an overall understanding of the purpose and content of the four Gospels, and to gain an overall understanding of the life of Jesus.

SCRIPTURE

Matthew 16:13-20; Luke 4:16-21; 5:1-11; John 20:30-31; Luke 24:44-49

HERE'S THE PLAN | **DO IT YOUR WAY**

OPTIONS	TIME (minutes)	PREPARATION	SUPPLIES
INITIAL CONNECTION			
A Greatest Player Ever	10	ask youth to bring sports cards with them	sports cards
B Superhuman Collage	10	gather comic books	comic books, poster board, scissors, glue
CONNECT WITH THE SESSION			
A Gospel Scavenger Hunt	15	make copies of Read Me "Outline of Things Found in the Gospels"	Bibles with subtitles, newsprint, paper, pencils
B Coat of Arms	15	make copies of page 16	construction paper, scissors, crayons
CONNECT WITH THE BIBLE AND THE FAITH COMMUNITY			
A Jesus' Life Outline	10	make copies of Apostle's Creed (page 15), YouthPage, & "Outline of Things Found in the Gospels"	YouthPage, copy of Apostle's Creed, newsprint, markers
B Palestine Map	10	make copies of map (page 37), and YouthPage	map of Palestine in Jesus' Day, YouthPage, colored markers
CONNECT WITH LIFE			
A House of Cards	10	bring playing cards to class	playing cards, Bibles
B Light to Dawn	10		Bibles, paper, pencils
CLOSING CONNECTIONS			
Prayer	2		

Desired Result:
To introduce the idea of greatness, and how we recognize it.
(Choose Option A or B.)

INITIAL CONNECTION

GREATEST PLAYER EVER

sports cards
*(**Allow 10 minutes.**)*

In advance, ask youth to bring several of their sports cards showing the greatest players in their sport. Ask them to be prepared to explain in class why that player might be considered the greatest.

SAY:

➤ **When we talk about greatness in sports figures, we do not have to know everything about them. For instance, we usually do not know where a great football player lives during the off season, whether he is married, or what he studied in college. We mainly determine greatness from statistics and performance. In the same way, the Gospels do not tell us every thing we might like to know about Jesus' life. Instead, they mainly tell us about the things he said and did, which prove that he was God's son.**

SUPERHUMAN COLLAGE

old comic books, poster board, scissors, glue
*(**Allow 10 minutes.**)*

Involve the students in making a collage for a superhuman, based on comic book heroes. Have a few students bring old comic books they don't mind cutting up to class. As a class, create a collage showing the things that make the comic book heroes superhuman.

After the collage is complete, place it in the room where everyone can see it.

SAY:

➤ **We can tell someone is superhuman by things they can do that the rest of us cannot; but usually, comic books do not tell us about the everyday lives of the characters. In the same way, the Gospels do not tell us everything we might like to know about Jesus' life in the way a biography would. Instead, the Gospels mainly tell us about the things he said and did, which prove that he was God's son.**

If you have enough time, you might want to discuss the following questions with the class.

ASK:

➤ **Suppose that this collage was about Jesus. What pictures of events in his life would you want to put on this collage that would show that he was superhuman?**

➤ **Superman can fly, and Spiderman can climb right up the sides of buildings. But, normal humans cannot do either of these things. If you think about the things that Jesus did during his life, do you feel that there is no way we can be like him? Or, should we try to be like him?**

CONNECT WITH THE SESSION

GOSPEL SCAVENGER HUNT

A

Desired Result:
To become familiar with the content of the Gospels. **(Choose Option A or B.)**

Before class, photocopy the "Outline of Things..." from page 34.

copies of "Outline..." on Read Me page, Bibles with subtitles, newsprint, paper, pencils ***(Allow 15 minutes.)***

Divide youth into small teams. Give each youth a Bible with subtitles (so that it is easy to find the beginning and end of various stories and sections of the Gospels). Explain that the Gospels are the books of Matthew, Mark, Luke, and John, and that they tell us about Jesus. Be sure everyone has found these four books in their Bible.

Briefly explain the outline. Give youth teams ten minutes to look through their Bibles for examples of the items on the outline. Explain that when they find an example in the Bible of a certain item on the outline, they should write the Scripture reference next to that item (for instance, they might write "Matthew 13:31-32" next to "parables"). The object is for them to find examples for as many different categories as possible. Tally up the score when time expires.

COAT OF ARMS

B

construction paper, scissors, crayons, YouthPage ***(Allow 15 minutes.)***

In this exercise, try designing a coat of arms for self and a coat of arms for Jesus. Explain that in olden days, families often had their own coat of arms. The symbols in this helped identify the unique characteristics of that family. Pass out the copies of the outline of the shield/coat of arms given on page 16, and ask that they divide it into four equal parts. Encourage them to be creative and use plenty of color. Ask them to draw a symbol (or at least write a word) in each part, as instructed below.

SAY:

➤ **In the upper left part, draw a symbol which shows some physical activity you like to do or would like to learn more about (for example, football, knitting, dancing).**

In the lower left part, draw a symbol which shows some mental activity you like to do or would like to learn more about (for example, math, science, computing, and so forth).

In the upper right part, draw a symbol which tells something about your

social life. It might be a picture of your family, or something that reminds you of one of your friends, or a symbol showing what you like to do when you get together with other people.

In the lower right part, draw a symbol that tells something about your religious life. For example, it might be a picture of your church, or something that reminds you of your favorite story in the Bible.

Next, give the youth a piece of construction paper, and have them create a coat of arms for Jesus in the same way. Ask them to use the story of Jesus on the YouthPage as a guide, or the Bible and their own understanding of Jesus' life. Allow volunteers to explain their own coat of arms, and to explain the coat of arms they made for Jesus.

CONNECT WITH THE BIBLE AND THE FAITH COMMUNITY

Desired Result:
To gain an overall understanding of the life of Christ.
(Choose Option A or B.)

A JESUS' LIFE OUTLINE

YouthPage, copy of Apostles' Creed, newsprint, markers
(Allow 10 minutes.)

Before class, copy the "Outline of things..." from the Get Ready page onto individual sheets for distribution to the class. The class will compare the events of Jesus' life to the Apostles' Creed.

Give youth a copy of the "Apostles' Creed," (page 15) or write it out on the newsprint and post it. Have youth compare it to a copy of "Things You Can Find in the Gospels" from the Get Ready page and "The Life of Christ" in the YouthPage. Make a list on the newsprint of "Things the Creed Leaves Out" and "Things the Creed Leaves In."

ASK:

- **Does the creed leave out anything about Jesus' life that you think is essential? What would you add to (or subtract from) the creed so that it covers everything that is most important to your faith?**

B PALESTINE MAP

map of Palestine in Jesus' day, YouthPage, colored markers
(Allow 10 minutes.)

Mark a map of Palestine in Jesus' day. Photocopy the map of Palestine in Jesus' day from page 37. Read through the story of Jesus' life on the YouthPage, marking the places on the map where Jesus lived during the various parts of his ministry. Invite youth to look through their Bibles for references to cities and then to locate these cities on the map, trying to tie them in to a particular portion of Jesus' overall life and movements.

CONNECT WITH LIFE

A

HOUSE OF CARDS

Give youth five minutes to build the tallest house of cards posssbile. Read Matthew 16:13-18 aloud to the class, stressing the rock foundation on which Jesus will build the church.

ASK:

➤ **What does Jesus mean by calling Peter the rock foundation?**

SAY:

➤ **Some people call a life which is not based on a solid faith a *house of cards* because it is likely to fall down just like a house of cards. However, Jesus called Peter's life "a rock upon which I will build my church," because Peter declared his faith in Jesus.**

ASK:

➤ **If your life had to be the foundation for the church, would you describe your faith as more like a house of cards or a rock foundation? If you wanted to grow closer to Jesus and strengthen your belief, what would you have to do to make that happen?**

B

Light to Dawn

SAY:

➤ **When someone "gets the point," we sometimes say, "The light dawned on them." In chapter 20 of John's Gospel, the light is the fact that Jesus rose from the dead and is the Messiah, the Son of God. Read the chapter and make a list of the people who get the point.**

After the youth have made the list, make sure that they put their name at the end of the list (since John 20:30-31 addresses the reader personally).

Desired Result:
To help youth understand that they can invite Christ into their lives, and this is the point Gospels are trying to make.
(***Choose Option A or B.***)

playing cards, Bibles
(*Allow 10 minutes.*)

Bibles, paper, pencils
(*Allow 10 minutes.*)

ASK:

- ➤ **What is the point that is supposed to "dawn on us" according to John 20:30-31?**
- ➤ **What difference did that point make in the lives of the people on your list?**
- ➤ **What difference does that point make in our lives?**

CLOSING CONNECTIONS

Desired Result:
To make a new commitment to follow Christ.

(***Allow 2 minutes.***)

PRAYER

Pray this prayer with your class, or make up your own prayer.

Dear Lord,

I confess that in some ways my life has been like a house of cards, because I often build it without thinking of you. I realize that I need you to be my rock foundation in life, and that you need my life to be like a rock foundation for your mission in the world. Please forgive me of my sins, and help me live for you in everything I do. Open my eyes to the light of your love, and help me draw closer to you each day; in Jesus' name we pray. Amen.

Read Me

THIS IS WHAT YOU NEED TO KNOW ABOUT THE TOPIC.

"Gospel" Good News!!!

The word *Gospel* was originally a translation of the Latin word *evangelium,* which means *preaching* or *proclamation*. Later it was changed into a shortened form of words, *God* + *spel,* which means *story*. Thus the word meant "God's story." Either way, it spells GOOD NEWS to Christians!

Matthew

Why Are There Four Gospels?

Actually there are more than four Gospels. Several ancient Gospels that scholars know about did not make it into the Bible we have today. There are at least five that we know of, including the Gospel of the Ebionites, the Gospel according to the Hebrews (also known as "The Jewish Gospel"), and the Gospel of Peter.

Luke

Mark

Of the four Gospels included in the Bible, Matthew, Mark, and Luke are known as Synoptic Gospels, because they share so much material in common. (Much of it is nearly word for word, meaning that one or the other deliberately copied parts of the other Gospels directly into his Gospel as he wrote it.) In fact, nearly all of Mark can also be found in either Matthew or Luke. If we lost Mark, we would still have most of our record of Jesus' life left intact.

John

John's Gospel is universally thought to be written fifty or so years later than the others. Scholars debate the exact order and date of the other three, but generally consider them to have been written within a generation of Jesus' life. In John, Jesus is portrayed giving much longer, more rambling speeches (in contrast to short sayings and parables in the other three). The theme of light and darkness is heavily emphasized in John. Jesus is the "light of the world;" and, gradually throughout the book, the light dawns on one person after another until, in the end of the book, the hope is that the light has dawned upon the reader as well!

GET READY

FAMOUS SCRIPTURES YOU MAY WANT TO LOOK UP IN CLASS OR SEND HOME IN WRITTEN FORM

All four Gospels are full of famous events.

Matthew 1-2; Luke 2:1-20 (Christmas stories)
Matthew 5-7 (Jesus' sermon on the mount)
Matthew 11:25-30 ("Come to me and I will give you rest")
Mark 12:28-34 (The Greatest Commandment)

Matthew

Luke 15:11-32 (The Prodigal Son Story)
Luke 22:14-20 (The Last Supper)
John 1:1-14 ("The Word became a human being...lived among us")
John 3:16 (the Scripture you see on signs at ball games!)
John 8:1-11 ("Let the one without sin throw the first stone")
John 11 (Jesus raises Lazarus; Jesus is "the resurrection and the life")
Jesus' death & resurrection (at the end of Matthew, Mark, Luke, and John)

Luke

An Outline of Things You Can Find in the Gospels

I. Jesus' life story
- A. His birth and early life
- B. His baptism, temptation, travels and other events
- C. His relationship with others
  1. his own family
  2. his disciples
  3. strangers, foreigners, sinners, and the outcast
  4. Jewish leaders
- D. His death and resurrection

II. Jesus' Teachings
- A. Parables and short sayings
- B. Teachings about the Old Testament laws
- C. Discussions with disciples and arguments with critics
- D. Other Statements of Jesus
  1. Prophecies about the future
  2. Warnings about false religious leaders
  3. Statements about his own life and purpose
- E. Scripture quotes
  1. By Jesus, to make a point about his message
  2. By the Gospel writers to make a point about Jesus

Mark

III. Miracles
- A. Healing the sick
- B. Nature miracles (walking on water, calming sea, multiplying food)
- C. Divine miracles (where God's unique powers show though, such as understanding people's thoughts before they speak, the transfiguration, casting out demons, etc.)
- D. Resurrections (people Jesus raised from the dead)

THE GOSPELS—THE BIG PICTURE
"THE LIFE OF CHRIST"

The story of Jesus' birth is only found in Matthew and Luke. They both include his family tree too, put in there to prove that Jesus was descended from King David (because the Messiah was supposed to be). Jesus' parents lived in the town of Nazareth, located in Galilee.

However, just before Jesus was born, the government forced everyone to travel to their home town for a census, and that is how Jesus was born in the town of Bethlehem (his father's home town). After fleeing to Egypt for a brief stay to avoid King Herod's plot to kill all baby boys, they moved back to Nazareth, where Jesus grew up and lived for the next thirty years. During that time, we know he grew up in a religious Jewish family, and he became a carpenter like his father, Joseph. That's about it. Everything else in the Gospels is about the last three years of his life—his public ministry.

Mark and John begin their Gospels at this point in the story. Anyway, John the Baptist began to baptize people in the river and tell people to get ready for the Messiah. When John the Baptist baptized Jesus, he started to figure out that Jesus was the Messiah everyone had been waiting for; but, not everyone had caught on yet. Jesus went out into the desert by himself for forty days, and was tempted to use his power in wrong ways; but he successfully resisted the temptations. Then he asked several fishermen and other not-too-churchy people to follow him. They did, and with them Jesus began a life of wandering from town to town. After an early rejection in his home town of Nazareth, he spent his time first in the region of Judea, and later back on his home turf of Galilee. As he went from place to place, he healed people who were sick and performed many other miraculous things. For instance, he fed a crowd of thousands with just a little bit of food, calmed a stormy sea, and even raised the dead a few times!

His miracles were never just for show. They always served the purpose of encouraging people to believe in God, and to believe that Jesus was God's son.

When Jesus taught, he usually spoke in short, catchy sayings or told memorable stories called parables. A parable is especially clever because it doesn't sound like what it's really about. It may sound like it's about someone planting grain; but, after you get home and start thinking about it, you suddenly realize that Jesus was telling you to

THE GOSPELS—THE BIG PICTURE
"THE LIFE OF CHRIST"

spread the Good News like a farmer spreads grain! Using parables meant people could easily remember what Jesus said.

Even though Jesus' disciples were with him all the time, they were slow to understand him. One real turning point was the day Simon Peter answered Jesus' question, "Who do you say that I am?," by declaring "You are the Messiah, the Son of the Living God!" It was the first time Peter "got it," and expressed his faith. Shortly after that, Jesus realized that God was calling him to go to Jerusalem, the center of Judaism, and that he would die there. Peter, sensing the danger, tried to stop Jesus, but Jesus went anyway. He even entered the city with a parade (Palm Sunday).

Jesus' activities caught the attention of the religious leaders, especially in Jerusalem, who felt threatened by his growing popularity. They were also angry that Jesus had exposed their moneymaking schemes by overturning the tables in the Temple, and repeatedly calling the leaders hypocritical. Several times they argued with him, tried to attack him, or schemed to discredit him with trick questions. Nothing seemed to work, so they plotted to kill him. They bribed Judas, one of Jesus' twelve disciples, to tell them where Jesus would be one evening. So, after having a last supper with his disciples (which we remember with Communion), Jesus was arrested in the Garden of Gethsemane.

His religious trial was a mockery, but they couldn't sentence him to die. The Roman government couldn't find any of their laws that Jesus had broken, but they gave in to public pressure and had Jesus crucified anyway (nailed to a wooden cross). He died hours later, and was buried. On Sunday morning his body was missing! Soon he made several appearances as the risen Christ to the disciples and others. They believed in him, and realized that God had been at work through everything that had happened. They began to preach to others and meet together, and to form the beginnings of the church. We will learn more about that next session!

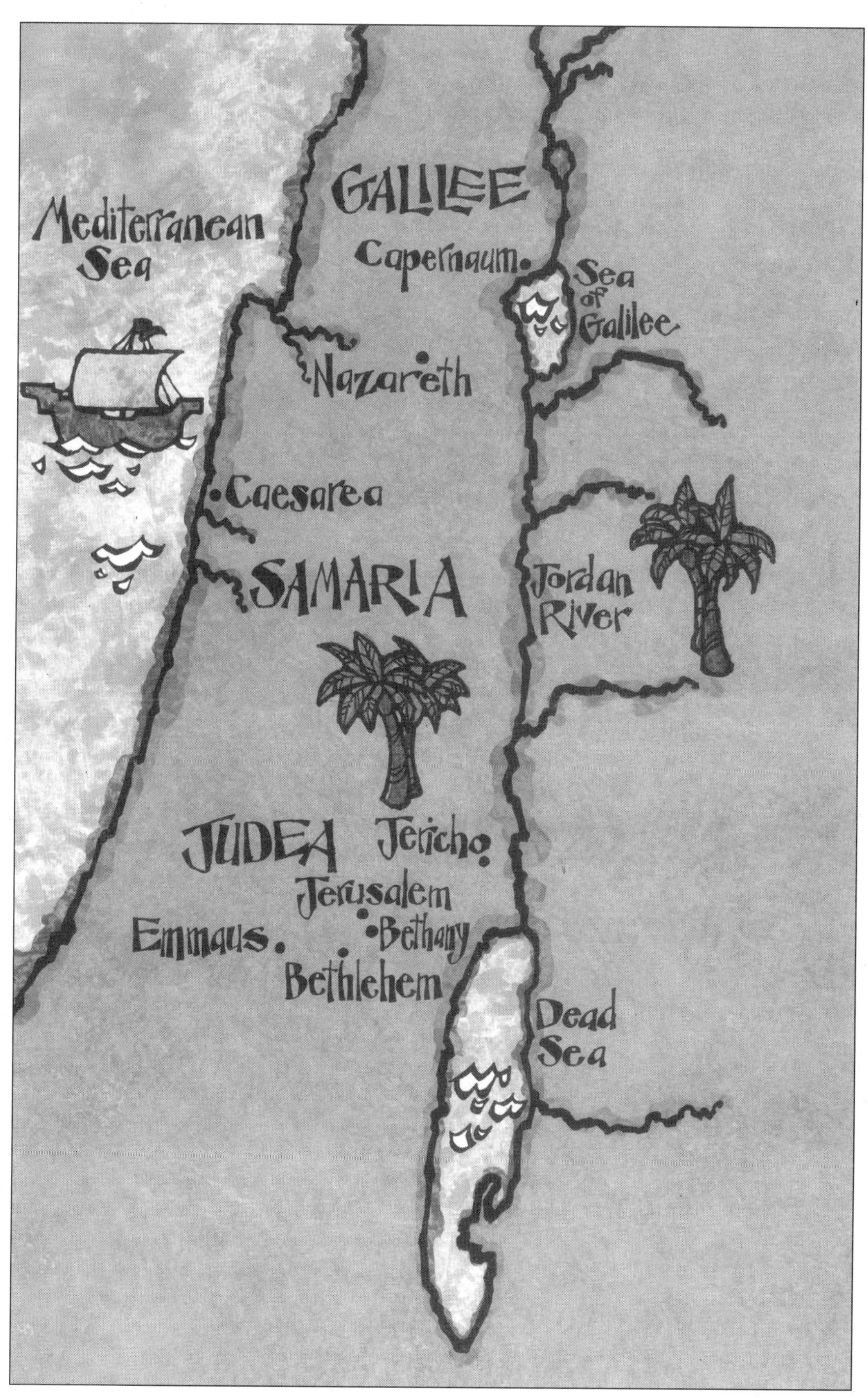
Mediterranean Sea
GALILEE
Capernaum
Sea of Galilee
Nazareth
Caesarea
SAMARIA
Jordan River
JUDEA
Jericho
Jerusalem
Bethany
Emmaus
Bethlehem
Dead Sea

SESSION 3:

THE NEW TESTAMENT LETTERS—THE BIG PICTURE

FOCUS

To gain an understanding of Peter, Paul, and the life of the early church.

SCRIPTURE

Acts 27:9-28:10; Philippians 3:12-14; 2 Corinthians 11:21-33; 12:7-10

HERE'S THE PLAN DO IT YOUR WAY

OPTIONS	TIME (minutes)	PREPARATION	SUPPLIES
INITIAL CONNECTION			
A Pack a Bag	10	gather items normally needed for a trip	small paper bags, assorted items
B Church History	15		paper, pencils
CONNECT WITH THE SESSION			
A New Testament Letter Collection	15-20	gather supplies	YouthPage, envelopes, construction paper, markers, Bibles with written introductions to books, commentaries
B Globe Spin	10	get globe; consider inviting someone to help provide information on missions	globe, information about your church's involvement in missions
CONNECT WITH THE BIBLE AND THE FAITH COMMUNITY			
A Paul's Travels	15-20	make copies of map on page 46; get map of North America; invite travel agent	Bible Atlas or map of Paul's travels, map of North America,
B Paul's Experiences	20	read Acts 16:16-34; collect supplies	Bibles, cassette, recorder, sound effect props as needed
CONNECT WITH LIFE			
A Evangelism Survey	10	interview minister or chairperson of Evangelism, or invite to participate in the class	newsprint, markers
B Write Missionary Letters	10-15		paper, pencils, Bibles
CLOSING CONNECTIONS			
Following in Paul's Footsteps	5		Bibles

INITIAL CONNECTION

A PACK A BAG

> **Desired Result:**
> To help youth begin to think about the mission of the church through a fun, team-oriented activity. **(Choose Option A or B.)**

small paper bags, assorted items
(Allow 10 minutes.)

Before class, gather a large selection of items for youth to pack into their paper sacks. If possible, select items that someone might want to take with them on a trip, or that could symbolize something to take. Items may include anything from rolls of toilet paper, to clothing, to games, to loose change. Be creative, humorous, and have a large variety of sizes and items to choose from. Include at least one Bible! Place the items on a table, and then cover the items with a cloth.

Divide the students into teams of two or three, and give each team a paper sack. Tell them that in two minutes they have to catch a plane for a long journey, and all they are allowed to take with them on this trip is whatever will fit into their paper bag. Uncover the table and say "Go!" Afterward, have youth volunteer to explain why they chose the things they did, and what other things they would have chosen if they had been available.

Point out the presence of the Bible.

SAY:

➤ **One of the main things the apostle Paul did in his life was travel from place to place. We don't know how many things he took with him, but he probably would have grabbed the Bible because he traveled in order to spread the gospel to other places.**

B CHURCH HISTORY

paper, pencils
(Allow 15 minutes.)

(NOTE: It would be a good idea to have alerted ahead of time several people with background knowledge of the church. They could be in conspicuous places and have copies of pamphlets, histories, and other relevant items to show the youth.)

When youth gather, divide them into two or more teams.

SAY:

➤ **I have a mystery I would like you to solve. The mystery is the story behind the existence of our local church. Whose idea was it to start this congregation? Why did they decide to start a new congregation, and when did they do it? Is this the original church building? If not, when and where was the original one built? Find out as much as you can about our church's beginnings. You can use the church library, read the cornerstone or plaques around the church building, ask some of the**

adults, or talk to the church historian. But you have only ten minutes. See how much information you can gather, and then come back to the classroom.

When youth return, pool your information to uncover the story behind how your church began.

CONNECT WITH THE SESSION

NEW TESTAMENT LETTER COLLECTION

A

Desired Result:
To recognize that the New Testament (after the story of Jesus' life in the Gospels) contains a record of the birth, faith, mission, and expansion of the Christian church.
(Choose Option A or B.)

YouthPage, envelopes, construction paper, markers, Bibles with written introductions to each book of the Bible, Bible commentaries
(Allow 15-20 minutes.)

SAY:

➤ **Most of the New Testament consists of letters from Paul or other early Christians to individuals or whole churches. Sometimes the writer or the intended recipient is unknown. Rather than being jumbled together randomly, there is a reason behind the order in which they are arranged in our Bible today. Let's see who can figure out the reasoning behind the arrangement, after everyone has completed gathering information about their assigned letters.**

Assign all the books of the New Testament (except for the four Gospels) to the class members, giving youth more than one book as needed. Obtain Bibles, such as *Today's English Version*, that have short paragraphs of introduction before each book of the Bible, or provide commentaries that do the same thing. Using these commentaries, have youth do the following for their assigned books.

1) On the envelope where the return address would normally go, write who the book/letter is from.

2) On the envelope, in the area where the mailing address would normally go, write the intended reader, whether individual or church.

(Note: Youth should complete the above two steps for all of their assigned books first. If time allows, they can go back and do step three.

3) Staple the envelope to a piece of construction paper. On the paper, write a sentence or two summarizing the content of that letter (for instance, "This is a letter warning against false teachers").

When all youth have finished, spread out on a table the books of the New Testament in the order in which they appear in the Bible.

Using the notes in the Read Me page for your background and guidance, help the students draw a few conclusions about the purpose and order of the New Testament books. Point out that after Acts (which continues the historical account following the Gospel stories), Paul's letters are arranged in order according to length (longest to shortest). The letters written by people other than Paul come next in the Bible, followed by Revelation, which is a vision of the end and a message of encouragement to those who are being persecuted. Hebrews is of unknown authorship, so it appears between Paul's letters and the letters written by other people.

B GLOBE SPIN

globe, information about your church's worldwide missions ***(Allow 10 minutes.)***

(Note: Possible guests to invite to this option might be your pastor or mission coordinator. They would be valuable resource persons to help explain your church's mission. The best source for current information on United Methodist missionaries would probably be the *Prayer Calender*. You can probably borrow one from your United Methodist Women's group. If not, call 1-800-305-9857 to order your own copy; cost is $6.50.)

Have one volunteer spin the globe, and a second volunteer stop it with her or his finger. If the finger is pointing to water, spin it again. When the volunteer's finger is on land, note the country. Using the mission resources you have gathered, find the answer to the question, "What missionaries or mission projects does our church have in this country? How can we support those efforts if we want to do so?" If you do not know or cannot find the answers, give the question as an assignment to one or more of the youth for next week. Repeat the globe spin at least three or four times.

SAY:

➤ **There are opportunities for mission everywhere in the world where people live. Even though some people say we should take care of our own needs before we worry about people in other parts of the world, we can be thankful that Paul did not feel that way. He felt it was important to spread the Christian message to everyone in the world, both locally and abroad. To him, mission meant talking about Jesus Christ to everyone he met, and he made it his goal in life to meet a lot of people.**

Desired Result:
To gain insight into Paul's life and travels, do a map study. **(Choose Option A or B.)**

CONNECT WITH THE BIBILE AND THE FAITH COMMUNITY

A PAUL'S TRAVELS

Bible Atlas or map of Paul's travels, map of North America) ***(Allow 15-20 minutes.)***

(Invite a travel agent, if possible, to help.) Before class, locate or create a large map of Paul's travels (small versions of three such maps exist in the Good News Bible and many other Bibles with maps; check also in a Bible Atlas). A map is also included in this issue on page 46. Hang it in the classroom next to a map of North America. If possible, invite a travel agent to lead this part of this activity. Tell him or her that you want the youth to picture the terrain Paul traveled through, and gain an understanding of the distances he traveled without modern conveniences in order to spread the gospel. It may be useful to compare distances with the distance between your city and other places familiar to your youth on the map of North America. Point out that Paul did not have a car, and make an estimate of how long it might have taken to get there on foot.

On the map, find the cities listed below to which Paul wrote letters. Point out that these are all cities which Paul visited, started churches in, and later wrote New Testament letters. (He also mentions many other cities and places, which are on the maps, but we have do not have his correspondence.)

Rome *Corinth* *Ephesus* *Philippi*

Colossae *Thessalonica* *the region of Galatia*

To help youth get an idea of the risk and daily hardships of Paul's travels, ask volunteers to read aloud the vivid account of Paul's shipwreck on his trip to Rome (Acts 27:9-28:10). Continue by reading Paul's list of some of the hardships he endured on his travels in 2 Corinthians 11:21-33 and 12:7-10.

PAUL'S EXPERIENCES

Bibles, cassette, tape recorder, sound effect props as needed ***(Allow 20 minutes.)***

Ahead of time, read through Acts 16:16-34, and collect props. As a class, make a tape recording of the sound effects of Acts 16:16-34. Assign all the speaking parts in Acts 16:16-34 to youth volunteers. Make an audio tape recording of the dialogue (not narration) found in that Scripture and any other sounds that your reading of it leads you to believe might have been heard during that experience. Be creative! Then listen to the results of your work!

You might want to do the following instead of or in addition to the above: To help youth get a broader idea of the risk and daily hardships of Paul's travels, ask volunteers to read aloud the vivid account of Paul's shipwreck on his trip to Rome (Acts 27:9-28:10). You might even want to make a second tape of portions of this experience!

Conclude by reading Paul's list of some of the hardships he endured on his travels in 2 Corinthians 11:21-33 and 12:7-10.

SAY:

➤ **Suppose Paul had never traveled, but instead had done his life's work in his home town of Tarsus? He would never have started churches in all those other parts of the world and written letters to the people, because he would never have met them. To see what a difference that would have made, pinch the pages of the New Testament Paul wrote between your fingers. See how much of the New Testament he wrote, just out of his concern for people in other places?**

CONNECT WITH LIFE

EVANGELISM SURVEY

A

Desired Result:
To apply the missionary zeal of Paul to the ministry of our local church by creating a new idea for your church's evangelism efforts.
(Choose Option A or B.)

newsprint, markers
(Allow 10 minutes.)

If possible, interview your minister or an evangelism committee member about what is being done through your church to reach people who are unchurched in your community, and to invite them to follow Christ. With them, or as a class, brainstorm ideas for getting a message about your faith to people who might not yet be exposed to your church. Write your ideas on the newsprint; then after class, have a designated secretary copy them neatly and submit them to your evangelism committee or other appropriate ruling body.

Consider some of the following questions/ideas:

1) Who currently receives your church newsletter? Who in town might not yet receive a newsletter from any church? What can you do about that?

2) If you could afford to put a message on a billboard on the highway near your town, what would you say? Can you find a way to afford it?

3) What experience does the average youth at your school have of church? What kind of people do you suppose they think "church people" are? How can you begin to change their impression?

4) To what extent have racial or economic barriers limited the group of people your church has become, and to whom you reach out?

5) How is your church making use of the Internet, and what opportunities could it offer your Sunday school class in communicating with youth and adults who are searching?

paper, pencils, Bibles
(Allow 10-15 minutes.)

WRITE MISSIONARY LETTERS

Find an address of your church's mission in one or more of the countries you found in your globe spin. If you did not choose the globe spin option, then give the youth a choice of at least two different world mission projects your church supports. Give class members time to write a letter asking what that mission does, what has been exciting to them lately, and what the class can do to support them. As replies come back, post them in the classroom.

CLOSING CONNECTIONS

Desired Result:
To feel the motivation of Paul and the early church leaders to share the gospel with others.

FOLLOWING IN PAUL'S FOOTSTEPS

Bibles
(Allow 5 minutes.)

ASK:

➤ **If Paul joined our church, what do you think he would do? Who would he go talk to in our town, and what would he say to them?**

SAY:

➤ **Remember that even though Paul did a lot of good, and we owe much of the New Testament to the fact that he took the time to write about his beliefs, he also experienced rejection and many other hardships. But Paul did not let rejection and failure stop him. He kept trying! We can keep trying too as we work to serve God like Paul did.**

Conclude by reading Philippians 3:12-14 aloud.

Read Me

THIS IS WHAT YOU NEED TO KNOW ABOUT THE TOPIC.

A Famous Letter Writer

An Epistle is a letter which, from the beginning, was probably intended to be read by a wider audience (such as a whole church). While it was written in the general format of personal correspondence of the day, its content is closer to a sermon or philosophical treatise. If one had been available, Paul almost certainly would have possessed a cellular phone and run up a terrible bill! But since no cellular service had yet come to the Holy Land, the Epistle was "the next best thing to being there." As Paul began churches across the face of what is today Europe, he could not be everywhere at once. Therefore, he wrote to maintain contact with the churches he had begun, answer their questions, and solve problems. The questions and problems can often be "read between the lines." For instance, there is no need to write an Epistle stressing the unity of all believers unless the church members in question are fighting amongst themselves.

Paul's letters were obviously kept, treasured, reread, copied, and shared with others.

Like our letters today, Epistles had a recognizable form, followed closely in the letters written by Paul and the other New Testament writers. While we close a letter by signing our name, they put the writer's name first, followed by the person/group to whom the letter is addressed, followed by a greeting, and then the body of the letter.

Letters were sent via a personal, trusted messenger traveling on foot. Paul's letters were obviously kept, treasured, reread, copied, and shared with others. Many of them came to have the status of Scripture. Many scholars think that Paul's longer Epistles are compilations of many letters, later reorganized into the form of a single, longer letter.

In any case, we are fortunate that for such a key person in Christian history, we have both a description of Paul's ministry, written by Luke in the book of Acts, and so many of Paul's writings.

Famous Scriptures in The New Testament Letters

- Acts 2 (Pentecost Story, the coming of the Holy Spirit)
- Romans 5 (How we are put right with God)
- Romans 8:31-39 (Nothing can separate us from his love)
- 1 Corinthians 13 (love chapter)
- Ephesians 4:1-16 (The unity of the body of Christ)
- Ephesians 6:10-20 (Put on the whole armor of God)
- James (practical applications of our Christian faith)
- 1 John 4:7-21 (God is love)
- Revelation 3:20 ("Behold, I stand at the door and knock")
- Revelation 21:1-8 (Jesus the Alpha and Omega, beginning and end)

MAP OF PAUL'S TRAVELS

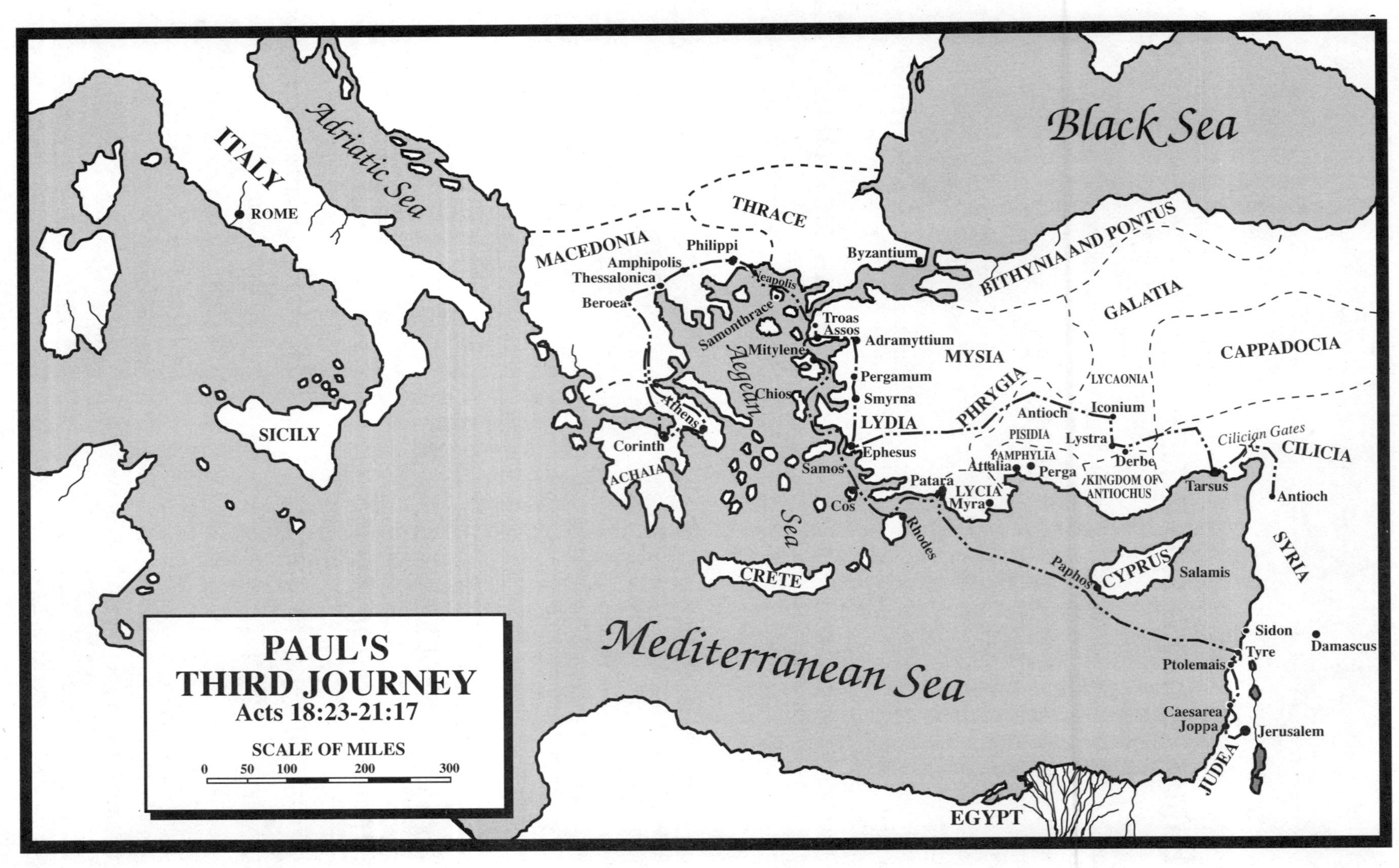

THE NEW TESTAMENT LETTERS— THE BIG PICTURE

AND NOW...THE REST OF THE STORY!!!

The New Testament begins with the story of Jesus (see session two "The Gospels—The Big Picture"), and then continues with the story of the early church. After the four Gospels, the next book is Acts. It is the history of the early church just after Jesus' death and resurrection. Luke wrote the Book of Acts as well as the Gospel of Luke. He is the only one of the Gospel writers who continued telling the story after the earthly life of Jesus—kind of like a movie sequel.

The book features two important New Testament characters, Peter and Paul. Peter was one of Jesus' disciples, and the one Jesus called the "rock on which he would build his church." Many people, probably including Peter himself and the other disciples, took this to mean Jesus wanted Peter to be the leader after Jesus' death. However, Paul's conversion after being confronted by the risen Christ, and his obvious zeal for leadership, meant that the early church had two strong leaders.

Strong leaders do not always agree and work in perfect harmony, so predictably, there was conflict. The central issue was whether new Christian converts who had not been Jewish before their conversion had to keep all the Jewish laws. In other words, are Christian followers still Jewish, or are they a different religion altogether?

Peter originally thought that they should keep the Jewish laws, and Paul disagreed. They settled their differences by dividing up the world into two mission fields. Peter tried to spread the faith in Jewish communities, and Paul sought converts in the Gentile (non-Jewish) world. In any case, the Book of Acts records the many actions and speeches of Peter and Paul and tells about the spread of the early church.

THE NEW TESTAMENT LETTERS—THE BIG PICTURE

The New Testament continues with a compilation of Paul's letters, roughly arranged from the longest to the shortest. Paul's letters are, in order, Romans, 1 & 2 Corinthians, Galatians, Ephesians, Philippians, Colossians, 1 & 2 Thessalonians, 1 & 2 Timothy, Titus, and Philemon. The name of each of Paul's letters comes from the person or church to whom he was writing (the churches at Rome, Corinth, Galatia, Ephesus, Philippi, Colossae, and Thessalonica; and to Timothy, Titus, and Philemon.)

It is unknown whether Paul wrote Hebrews (but most scholars do not think he did). The intended audience is also quite unclear. Thus, Hebrews is placed between Paul's letters and the letters of other New Testament letter writers.

The next group of New Testament books carries the name of their respective authors: James, Peter, John (almost certainly not the author of John's Gospel), and Jude.

Revelation, also written by someone named John (but apparently not the Gospel writer or Epistle writer), is an example of "apocalyptic" writing. The only other example of this type of writing in the Bible is the Old Testament book of Daniel. Apocalyptic writing was originally intended for people undergoing persecution. The need for secrecy helps explains the reason for the heavy symbolism (for example, the "seven lamps" probably mean the churches, since churches are the light for the world). The purpose of this type of writing is to encourage people to remain faithful in spite of the threatening, hostile atmosphere in which they live. It conveys a terrifying picture of the battle between good and evil, painting in graphic images the destruction of evil and the glorious reward of those who persevere to the end, thus motivating people not to abandon their faith even when under the threat of death.

FAMILY

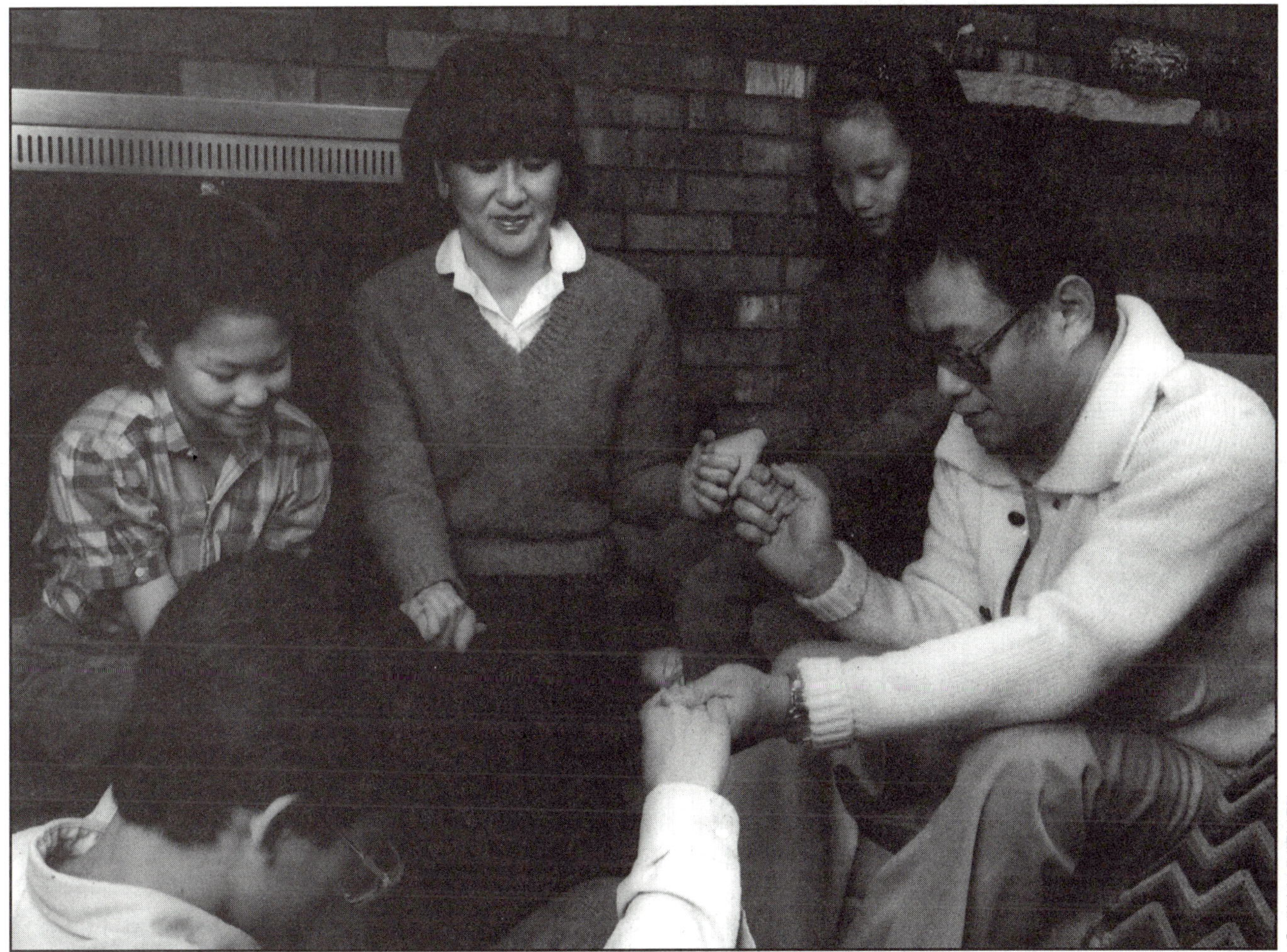

© JIM WHITMER

SESSION 1: IS MY FAMILY NORMAL?
SESSION 2: WHY ALL THESE FAMILY TRADITIONS?
SESSION 3: FAMILY OF GOD

Purpose

In this unit, youth will examine their relationship with their own family and with the family of God.

This Is Not Junk Mail!

IT'S IMPORTANT STUFF FROM YOUR TEENAGER'S SUNDAY MORNING LEADER

YOUR FAMILY

Does it seem as if your family lives in a fish bowl, and everyone is judging how good a job you are doing in raising your kids? Or does it seem that your family is separated from others and doesn't really have much contact with people other than just what is absolutely necessary through work and school? Or does everything actually seem to work out pretty smoothly because your family cares about one another and tries to work out any problems before they become crisis situations? Is your family different from what you remember growing up? Have you ever wondered if your family was normal?

Many youth live with one of the following situations: two working parents, a single parent, a guardian, adoptive parents, or blended families. Normal is not a particularly helpful word when it comes to measuring families of the late 1990's. In order for youth to grow up with loving caring attitudes toward their family members and other people, they must find these attitudes in their own family. Youth spend much more time with their families than they do at church. Parents need to live out the virtues and values they hope to find in their children. Remember that Paul could see the spiritual training that Timothy gained from his mother and grandmother (2 Timothy 1:3-7). Joshua told the crowd that his family would be faithful to God, and he challenged others to live the same way (Joshua 24:14-16). Are there ways your family has recently been an influence to other families?

Growing a Family Isn't as Easy as Growing a Flower

If you plant a flower and care for it properly, you will know pretty much how it will turn out. Or will you? Of course, there are the variables of mislabeled packages, fickle sunshine, sudden storms, uneducated-but-trying-to-help-weed-pullers, and digging dogs.

It isn't easy growing a faithful family in our culture today is it? Be aware of the issues of time management, money, truthfulness, worship, caring for others, and different activities that might bring your family closer together. What tends to alienate the members of your family or to keep you from having enough time to bond and care for each other? Even good activities can sometimes take away from family growth and togetherness. Ask yourselves if your children really need to be involved in too many activities outside of the home? Which activities are most important? Talk about which traditions are the most meaningful to you and meaningful in your family history. Find the time for the whole family to support each member in activities that will mean the most to them.

Hallelujah!

IDEAS FOR PEOPLE WHO PLAN WORSHIP

WORSHIPING WITH OUR GIFTS

The way we treat our church family is a reflection of our love for God. As you lead worship during the next few weeks, focus some attention on family issues. Be sure to mention how families come in all shapes and sizes, and remind your congregation that God does not measure a family by the make-up of members who are in the family, but by how the members love God, one another, and other people.

During the prayer time, remember to pray for the families in the church who make up the family of God in this place. If there are any special needs in your surrounding family, or church family, that the youth group or Sunday school classes could easily support, let them know how they can provide some assistance.

FAMILY COMMITMENT SERVICE

When people get married, they make vows to each other in front of God and the church family. Why not have a service of love and commitment for families? Make this a special service for families who want to make commitments and faith promises to each other. This might be something that will especially help blended families and hurting families find some healing and support from their church family.

FOR MUSIC MINISTRY

Happy the Home When God Is There
Help Us Accept Each Other (Can be read or sung.)
Praise God, from Whom All Blessings Flow
(The Doxology)
Blest Be the Tie That Binds
We Are the Church

SCRIPTURE READINGS

The Bible speaks of many families who seek to follow God, yet often find themselves in crisis situations. Sometimes the trials come because the families have disobeyed God's directives. Sometimes the crisis comes even when the people are faithful to God. Here are some passages which reflect the diversity of family situations in Scripture.

Genesis 7:6-10, 9:8-16 *(Noah and his family go on a cruise. Their vacation gets rained out, but they are the first people to see a rainbow.)*

Genesis 21:1-7 *(Elderly parents, Abraham and Sarah, have a child.)*

Genesis 22:1-14 *(Abraham and Isaac take a father and son trip to a place of worship. How could this be a foreshadowing of the crucifixion?)*

Genesis 25:23-28 *(Brothers who have different interests and personalities, one the hunter and the other a shepherd.)*

Genesis 37:3-4,17-20 *(Jealous brothers plan to get rid of the favorite son.)*

Exodus 4:18-20 *(Moses moves his family to the mission field in Egypt.)*

Exodus 12:21-28 *(The lamb is killed and the blood is the symbol which saves the families of God's people. Then they take a church/family trip that only lasts forty years—someone must have forgotten the map.)*

Joshua 24:14 *(Joshua's family serves the Lord and asks others to do the same.)*

Ruth 1:1-16 *(Naomi's husband and sons die.)*

Matthew 2:11-14 *(Joseph has to suddenly move his family to another place.)*

Luke 2:41-52 *(Every year at Passover, Jesus' family went to Jerusalem for the celebration.)*

Ephesians 3:14-19 *(Families take name and image from God.)*

2 Timothy 1:2-7 *(Timothy learned about faith from his grandmother and mother.)*

1 Peter 2:4-10 *(As living stone we build the family of God.)*

1 John 4:7-16 *(Live in harmony with one's neighbors.)*

Miscellany

IDEAS FOR TEACHERS

YOUNGER YOUTH

Younger youth will have varied experiences with family, traditions, and church. They might not have had the opportunity to be in many situations where they are responsible for the success or failure of an activity or tradition. They will have identified themselves with being in a normal or an abnormal or dysfunctional family.

Younger youth will need shorter, more active lessons and more object lessons. Discussion activities should be well structured. Put discussion questions up on the board or repeat them to keep younger youth on task.

Younger youth may not have as much confidence in being a part of the family of God as older teens. On the other hand, they might have very big ideas, and may need guidance to look at situations realistically. How can they be a witness as a member of the family of God without feeling too weird?

OLDER YOUTH

Older youth, through some experience, will hold stronger opinions about their own families and what it means to be a member of the family of God.

Since they have had more experiences, older youth will have a much stronger sense of whether their family situation is normal or average. Many will already have some idea of what kinds of traditions they like and will keep to celebrate for the rest of their lives.

> Feeling alienated is a familiar situation for many youth.

Older youth can benefit a great deal from small group discussion. They diverge from the topic easily, though, so repeat the discussion questions or write them on a board or sheet of paper.

FAMILY OF GOD

Many youth feel out of place, awkward, or like misfits even when they are not specifically acting like Christians. They try hard to fit in with the crowd as they seek out their own identities. Feeling alienated is a familiar situation for many youth.

> Let youth know they are not going to be perfect by always knowing how to witness to friends and family.

Talking with others about Jesus can be a natural part of being a friend. Hopefully, talking about God and living out their faith is a part of their family life. Use a little extra effort to draw out shy youth for their opinions and participation, for they can have terrific family stories and traditions to tell.

SESSION 1:

IS MY FAMILY NORMAL?

FOCUS

To realize that since families come in different shapes and sizes, youth should look for attributes such as love and caring to describe family, rather than terms such as normal.

SCRIPTURE

Genesis 7:5-8; 25:23-28; 37:3-4,17-20; Exodus 2:1-10; 4:18-20; Judges 13:24-14:3; Ruth 1:1-16; Matthew 2:11-14

HERE'S THE PLAN | DO IT YOUR WAY

OPTIONS	TIME (minutes)	PREPARATION	SUPPLIES
INITIAL CONNECTION			
Choose the Real Family	5	cut pictures representing different kinds of families from several magazines, and make poster	posterboard, tape, marker, paper, pencils, pictures
CONNECT WITH THE SESSION			
A Family Poll	10	obtain supplies before class	board & chalk or newsprint and markers
B Choices	10	make copies of YouthPage	YouthPage, paper, pens
CONNECT WITH THE BIBLE AND THE FAITH COMMUNITY			
A Families of the Bible	12	read the Scriptures before class so you are familiar with the families	Bibles for each class member, pencils, paper
B The Family of the Week	12	read the Scriptures before class so you are familiar with the families	Bibles for each group
CONNECT WITH LIFE			
My Family Shield	15	make copies of YouthPage; research family shilelds and crests; obtain supplies	YouthPage and colored pencils or crayons
CLOSING CONNECTION			
God's Shield	6	draw a shield on a large piece of paper and tape it to the wall	markers, tape, and a large piece of paper with a shield drawn on it

INITIAL CONNECTION

CHOOSE THE REAL FAMILY

Desired Result:
To break the ice.

posterboard, tape, and marker, pictures cut from several magazines representing different kinds of families, paper, pencils **(*Allow 5 minutes.*)**

Before class begins, tape several pictures of different kinds of families, preferably from all around the world, to a poster board or a large sheet of paper; hang it where the students can see it. Write a number beside each picture. When class begins, tell the youth to choose the picture they think represents a normal family and to write the number on their piece of paper. Beside the numbers they choose, they must write why they think this is a normal family. After they have finished, ask for volunteers to tell why they chose certain pictures as normal families.

SAY:

➤ **There are no right or wrong answers in this activity. Families come in many different shapes and sizes. Some families have two parents, some only one. Some families are found in group homes, and some have foster parents. Some families have grandparents or an aunt or uncle as the guardian of the children. The church is also a family for many people who live alone.**

CONNECT WITH THE SESSION

Desired Result:
To help youth think about their own family.
(Choose Option A or B.)

A FAMILY POLL

board & chalk or newsprint and marker **(*Allow 10 minutes.*)**

ASK the following questions and record the verbal answers on the board or newsprint.

➤ **How is your family like other families?**

➤ **How is your family different from other families?**

➤ **Would you consider your family to be normal? Why or why not?**

B CHOICES

YouthPage, paper, pens **(*Allow 10 minutes.*)**

Pass out the YouthPages and ask the youth to read North's story.

ASK:

➤ **How was North's story like or unlike your situation in your family?**

➤ **What would you do if you were in North's place?**

Ask the youth to write their own family story or autobiography from the perspective of their place in their own family.

Discuss how each member of a family is important to that family.
ASK:

➤ **How are you important to your family?**

➤ **What do you like about your family?**

➤ **What would you change if you could?**

➤ **What do the other persons in your family do to help make your house a family home?**

CONNECT WITH THE BIBLE AND THE FAITH COMMUNITY

FAMILIES OF THE BIBLE

A

Desired Result: Youth will learn that families in the Bible were not always perfect, but God can use any of us to make a difference in the world. ***(Choose Option A or B.)***

Bibles, paper, pencils ***(Allow 12 minutes.)***

Before class, write out the Scriptures listed below on bits of paper, or copy them onto the board. Pass out Bibles to every class member and assign each student a passage from the list.

SAY:

➤ **Families are discussed many times in the Bible. Let's read some passages that show how very different these families are. Some families are dysfunctional—affected by sibling rivalry—and some seem to be harmonious.**

➤ **After you read the passage, summarize the kind of family in your own words.**

Genesis 7:5-8 (Noah, his wife, their sons and their son's wives go on a long voyage together.)

Genesis 21:1-7 (Elderly parents, Abraham and Sarah, have a child.)

Genesis 25:23-28 (Brothers who have different interests and personalities, one the hunter and the other a shepherd.)

Genesis 37:3-4,17-20 (Jealous brothers plan to get rid of the favorite son.)

Genesis 48:8-11 (A grandfather joyously finds his long lost son and two grandsons as well.)

Exodus 2:1-10 (Moses, son of a slave, was adopted and grew up in the royal family.)

Exodus 4:18-20 (Moses moves his family to the mission field in Egypt.)

Joshua 24:14 (Joshua's family serves the Lord and asks others to do the same.)

Ruth 1:1-16 (Naomi's husband and two sons die.)

Judges 13:24-14:3 (Family facing the breaking of marriage traditions.)

Matthew 2:11-14 (Joseph has to suddenly move his family to another place.)

2 Timothy 1:2-7 (Timothy learned about faith from his grandmother and mother.)

ASK the class to discuss the following questions:

➤ **What can you know about the family in this passage?**

➤ **What happens in the passage you read?**

➤ **Is this a normal family?**

➤ **How was this family important to God and God's people?**

ASK what they think about the following statement in the light of the Scriptures they have just read.

➤ **God only asks normal or loving families to love him, do his will, and carry out his plans.**

B THE FAMILY OF THE WEEK

Bible for each group
(Allow 12 minutes.)

Divide the class into three or four groups. Give each group one of the following passages and ask them to figure out all they can about the family in the Scripture.

How would their story be told if it was the movie of the week? Let the groups write a plot for a TV movie using modern people and situations. Let the groups tell about their creative modernization of the story. Ask the class to discuss how these families are different and similar to us today. (If you have a small class, choose specific passages to use; and let the youth work as individuals or partners. If you have a large class and would like to, assign all the passages.)

Genesis 7:5-8 (Noah and his wife and their sons and their son's wives go on a long voyage together.)

Genesis 25:23-28 (Brothers who have different interests and personalities, one the hunter and the other a shepherd.)

Genesis 37:3-4,17-20 (Jealous brothers plan to get rid of the favorite son.)

Exodus 2:1-10 (Moses, son of a slave, was adopted and grew up in the royal family.)

Exodus 4:18-20 (Moses moves his family to the mission field in Egypt.)

Judges 13:24-14:3 (Family facing the breaking of marriage traditions.)

Ruth 1:1-16 (Naomi had husband and two adult, married sons die.)

Matthew 2:11-14 (Joseph has to suddenly move his family to another place.)

CONNECT WITH LIFE

MY FAMILY SHIELD

Desired Result:
Youth will identify the good traits of their family.

YouthPage, colored pencils or crayons, paper
(Allow 15 minutes.)

Before class, get copies of some family shields or coats of arms to show as examples. Check the library or the Internet for this information. An art supply store might have an inexpensive book about creating a coat of arms. If you don't have a family crest, some of the families in your church will have their family colors and a shield. Ask for help from the parents to gain samples of this historic art form.

SAY:

➤ **In long ago times families were often separated for long periods of time by travel, war, and natural disasters. Long lost relatives and extended family members could recognize each other by their colors, crests, shields, and coats of arms. The symbols would be representative of the deeds, honors, or philosophies of the family line.**

If you were to design a family shield for your family, what would it look like? If you have seen your family crest, you might want to design it differently for this activity. What symbols are important to your family? What is your family famous for? What motto would be your family philosophy? Take some time and design your family shield on your Youth-

Page. You may include in the design family memories from the past or hopes for the future of your family.

Allow about seven minutes for youth to work on this.

ASK:

- **Was it easy or difficult to decide what to put on your shield to best represent your family?**

- **Would it be easy to be the head of a household?**

- **Did you find that you wanted to put too much on the shield? Or did you find that you did not have many ideas of what you wanted to include?**

- **What symbols did you decide were the most important for your family? the least important?**

- **What symbols do you think God would say are the most important?**

Invite any youth who want to say more about their family shield, or more about their hopes for the future to do so now.

CLOSING CONNECTION

GOD'S SHIELD

markers, large piece of paper with a shield drawn on it taped to the wall
(Allow 6 minutes.)

Ahead of time, draw the outline of a shield on a large sheet of paper or poster board. Ask the class to think for a minute about how God might design a shield for a Christian family. Invite the youth to add symbols that represent a Christian family on the shield on the YouthPage. As they are drawing on the shield, read passages like Ephesians 5:21; 6:1-3, 4, 10-17. After they complete and compare their personal shields. Encourage them to draw symbols on the shield; keep the shield on the wall as a reminder.

SAY:

- **Families come in all shapes and sizes. We shouldn't try to measure a normal family by what it looks like to other people in our society. God measures a family by how the members care about others. Challenge your family to make a difference in the world for God. God can use any family whose members open their hearts to the possibilities of ministry. Is your family normal? I hope not!**

Close in prayer.

Lord, help us to put our trust in you, and not in things or status symbols of the world. We thank you for the gifts you have given us, especially for the gift of family. Help our families to seek first your kingdom. Amen.

Read Me

THIS IS WHAT YOU NEED TO KNOW ABOUT THE TOPIC.

There are many ideas about what a normal family is.

WHY THIS UNIT FOR SUNDAY SCHOOL?

Family can be a sensitive subject for adults and youth. Debates about family values are popular in our culture. There are many ideas about what a normal family is. There are few clear examples of strong families in the media and on TV. Yet, if we are going to train youth to be good Christian disciples, then we cannot ignore the issues of growing strong, loving, courageous families.

As youth mature, they will naturally spend less time with their family. Therefore it is important that they have found their values and virtues in their families and church to help them meet the challenges and temptations they will face in life.

KEY IDEAS IN THIS UNIT

- The focus is on family.
- A family can love and be courageous enough to stand for the gospel of Jesus Christ.
- A family can find meaningful traditions that involve everyone and help each other remember what is really important to them.
- Each family can find love in the church family--which cares enough to reach out to all who are hurting, homeless, hungry, lonely, or lost.

TODAY'S YOUTH

Many youth today do not have a unified, identified cause. Youth of past generations have had uniting causes that gave them identity. This generation seems to have too many causes to deal with, thus they have not united together in one cause. This tends to leave youth out there working for themselves. Selfishness is one of the main vices of this generation.

Part of your role as church school teacher is to help youth develop an identity as Christians. Christians are to be Christ-like in all aspects of life, including the way in which they approach their role in their own family. Some youth in your class will have the examples of what it is like to be a part of a faithful and godly family. Others will not.

Many denominations have an opinion on the definition of family. The paragraph on the next page is the United Methodist definition.

IN THE MEDIA

It is difficult to find a TV family with whom we in the church can identify. Many TV parents tend to be self-absorbed in career with no time for the kids, or else the parents act stupid, uncaring, and mean-spirited toward their family and others. The kids in the TV families tend to be selfish brats, always trying to outsmart family and social rules, willing to do anything to fit in with a crowd or a date, or total loners left out of life. Of course, all this rarely makes for dramatic and comedy situations that are actually sensitive and funny without leaving the family sacrificed for the sake of the ratings. How many times do youth need to see the same kind of manipulative scenarios before they imitate and embrace this way of behavior?

"**The Family**—We believe the family to be the basic human community through which persons are nurtured and sustained in mutual love, responsibility, respect, and fidelity. We understand the family as encompassing a wider range of options than that of the two-generational unit of parents and children (the nuclear family), including the extended family, families with adopted children, single parents, stepfamilies, and couples without children. We affirm shared responsibility for parenting by men and women and encourage social, economic, and religious efforts to maintain and strengthen relationships within families in order that every member may be assisted toward complete personhood."

IS MY FAMILY NORMAL?

Not many families are composed of two children with a dad who goes to the office each day and a mom who stays home to care for the kids and the house. So what is a normal family anyway? Well, there really isn't a perfect answer to that question. Most Christian families struggle with money, time management, education, household chores, questionable TV and other media values, sports or other extracurricular activities, church activities, and where to go on vacation.

If your family struggles with these things, you are probably normal. Make a short list of the things about your family you think are normal and then make a list of the things you think might set your family aside from the average family. Check the things you think are good that set your family apart from being average family.

NORMAL	SET APART
1.__________	1.__________
2.__________	2.__________
3.__________	3.__________
4.__________	4.__________
5.__________	5.__________
6.__________	6.__________

N·O·R·T·H ??????

Did you see *North*, that movie about a kid who got tired of his family and decided to find a new family? He auditioned or interviewed several potential families and had a difficult time finding the perfect family. Find someone who has seen this movie about this prodigal child, and find out what happened to North in the end.

What would you look for if you could choose your family? Write a want ad in the space below describing your ideal family.

Design a shield using the symbols that best represent your family. Add a motto or Scripture verse for your family.

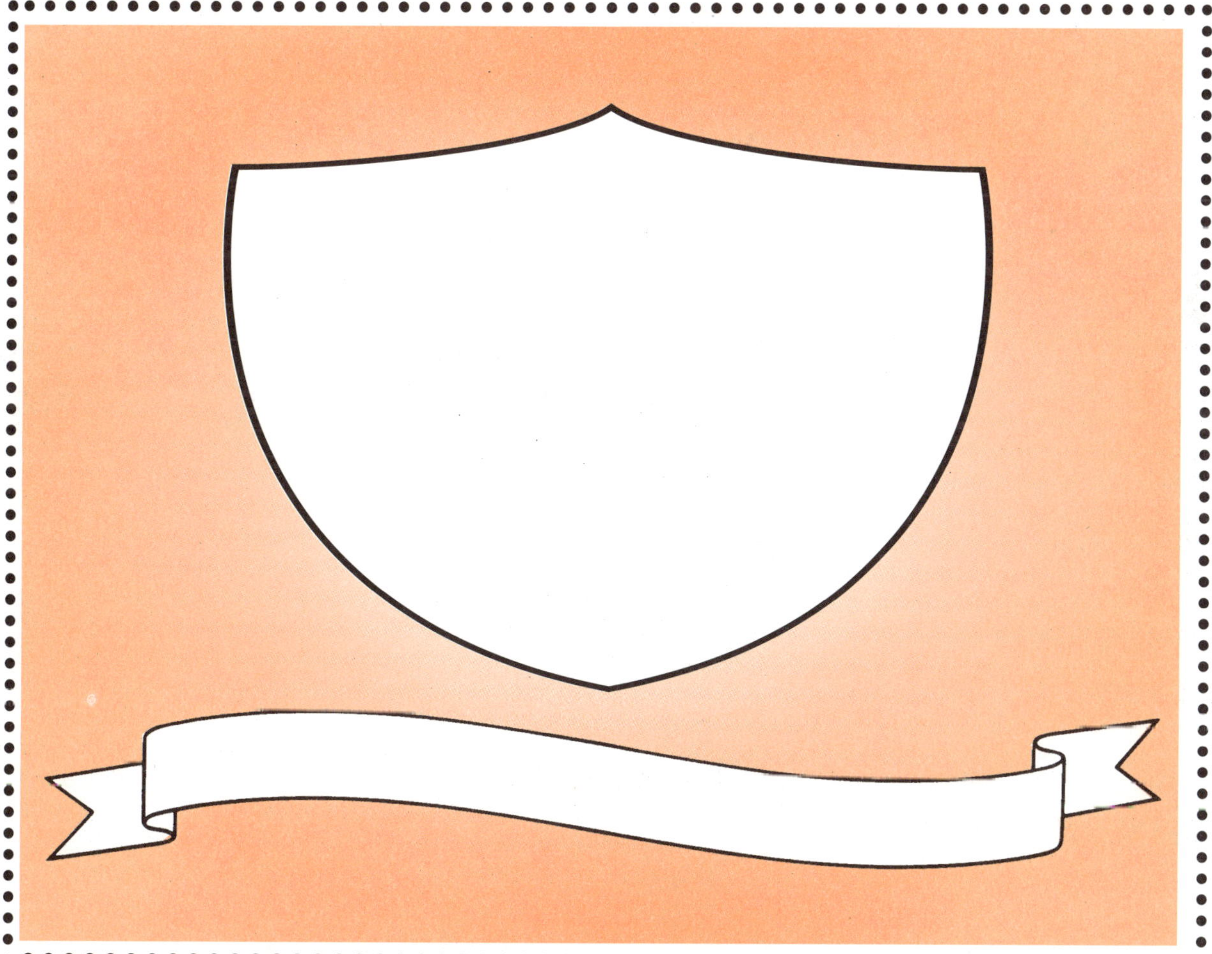

SESSION 2:

WHY ALL THESE FAMILY TRADITIONS?

FOCUS

To examine how traditions can be fun and meaningful in a family.

SCRIPTURE

Luke 2:41-52

HERE'S THE PLAN | DO IT YOUR WAY

OPTIONS	TIME (minutes)	PREPARATION	SUPPLIES
INITIAL CONNECTION			
The Best Thing My Family Ever Did	6	make copies of YouthPage	YouthPage & pencils or pens
CONNECT WITH THE SESSION			
A Traditions	7-10	make copies of YouthPage	YouthPage
B What's a Tradition?	5-7	tape large piece of paper to classroom wall	marker, tape, paper
CONNECT WITH THE BIBLE AND THE FAITH COMMUNITY			
A The Birth of a Tradition	12	secure supplies before class; write discussion questions on paper and post for small groups to see	large piece of paper, marker, and Bible for each group
B Where Is Your Tradition?	10		Bibles
C Active Traditions	15		Bibles
CONNECT WITH LIFE			
A What's My Part?	10		chalkboard & chalk or newsprint and markers
B My Family Traditions	10	make copies of YouthPage	YouthPage, pencils
CLOSING CONNECTION			
Prayer Time	5-7	make copies of YouthPage	YouthPage, pencils

INITIAL CONNECTION

THE BEST THING MY FAMILY EVER DID

Ahead of time, take a few minutes to write down the best thing your family ever did. As youth gather, give each one a YouthPage and a pencil. **ASK:**

➤ **What is the best thing your family ever did?**

Have youth write their answers on the YouthPage. Invite class members to tell about the best thing their family ever did. As they tell the class about their experiences, **ASK:**

➤ **What makes this the best thing your family ever did?**

➤ **Was it fun, meaningful, emotional, educational, spiritual?**

➤ **Is this activity now a tradition with your family?**

If you care to, tell the group what you wrote about your family's experience.

Desired Result:
To break the ice and begin thinking about traditions.

YouthPage, pencils or pens
(Allow 6 minutes.)

CONNECT WITH THE SESSION

TRADITIONS

Give the youth a couple of minutes to read and think about the section on their YouthPage entitled "Traditions."

ASK:

➤ **What family activities do you enjoy the most?**

➤ **What activities or trips seemed like a good idea when you planned them, but didn't really work out that well?**

➤ **What activities caused the most family conflict?**

➤ **What activities promoted family togetherness and were enjoyed by the whole family?**

➤ **Why are traditions important to any family?**

Desired Result:
To examine how traditions are important to a family.
(Choose Option A or B.)

YouthPage
(Allow 7-10 minutes.)

large piece of paper taped to wall, marker
(Allow 5-7 minutes.)

WHAT'S A TRADITION?

B

Let a volunteer make three columns (actual traditions, why it's a tradition, why it's important) on the large piece of paper and record important points of the class discussion.

ASK:

- **Which of the family activities that we talked about are actually traditions in your family?**
- **What makes something a tradition?**
- **Why are traditions important to any family?**

CONNECT WITH THE BIBLE AND THE FAITH COMMUNITY

Desired Result:
To learn about some family traditions in the Bible.
(Choose Option A, B, or C.)

THE BIRTH OF A TRADITION

A

large piece of paper, marker and tape, Bible for each group
(Allow 12 minutes.)

Before class begins, copy the questions listed below on posterboard or newsprint. Tape the posterboard where everyone can see it.

Divide the youth into three or four pairs, or small groups if you have a large class. Assign each group one of the following Scriptures. Ask them to answer the questions about their passage. Allow time for the small groups to tell the class what they decided.

Genesis 7:6-10; 9:8-16 (Noah and his family go on a cruise. Their vacation gets rained out, but they are the first people to see a rain bow.)

Genesis 22:1-14 (Abraham and Isaac take a father and son trip to a place of worship. How could this be a foreshadowing of the crucifixion?)

Exodus 12:21-28 (The lamb is killed and the blood is the symbol which saves the families of God's people. Then they take a church/family trip that only lasts forty years—someone must have forgotten the map.)

Luke 2:41-52 (Every year at Passover, Jesus' family went to Jerusalem for the celebration.)

What do you think you would say if you were there in that situation?

What does this story tell about how God wants us to remember traditions?

What traditions do you have in your family that are like what happens in this passage? How are you family traditions different?

WHERE IS YOUR TRADITION?

Bibles
(*Allow 10 minutes.*)

Pass out Bibles so that youth can read along and refer to the passage. It is helpful if all class members are reading from the same translation, but it may add to the discussion if some youth notice differences in the text of their Bibles. Try to find a copy of "The Cotton Patch Version of the Gospel" as well. Read the following passage out loud together as a class.

Luke 2:41-52 (Every year at Passover, Jesus' family went to Jerusalem for the celebration.)

ASK:

- **Why would you consider going to Jerusalem for the Passover Festival to be a tradition for Jesus' family?**
- **What are your family traditions that are similar to this? (Are there others beside Christmas and Easter?)**

ACTIVE TRADITIONS

Bibles
(*Allow 15 minutes.*)

Divide the class into four groups and assign each group one of the following passages. Give them a few minutes to decide how they would act out this story. Then let them present their drama to the class. Traditions are frequently acted out by those who remember an important event. We often see Christmas and Easter plays in our churches each year. We pray before a meal and remember to thank Jesus for blessings.

Genesis 7:6-10; 9:8-16 (Noah and his family go on a cruise. Their vacation gets rained out, but they are the first people to see a rain bow.)

Genesis 22:1-14 (Abraham and Isaac take a father and son trip to a place of worship. How could this be a foreshadowing of the crucifixion?)

Exodus 12:21-28 (The lamb is killed and the blood is the symbol which saves the families of God's people. Then they take a church/family trip that only lasts forty years. Someone must have forgotten the map.)

Luke 2:41-52 (Every year at Passover, Jesus' family went to Jerusalem for the celebration.)

ASK:

➤ **Does this Scripture remind you of any particular kind of tradition?**

➤ **Why celebrate traditions?**

➤ **What is a good way to celebrate a meaningful tradition?**

CONNECT WITH LIFE

Desired Result: Youth will examine their family traditions. (***Choose Option A or B.***)

WHAT'S MY PART?

board or newsprint and markers ***(Allow 10 minutes.)***

SAY:

➤ **Christians believe that families need to spend time together so that family members learn to love and care for one another and sense the ties that bind them together. Family traditions bring the family together to celebrate or remember the times which are meaningful and important to the family. What part do you (or could you) play in helping to celebrate or observe traditions and special activities in your family?**

Have the youths turn to partners and tell each other what kind of traditions they want to start or become more involved in within their families.

Now invite class members to tell the whole group what tradition interested them.

MY FAMILY TRADITIONS

YouthPage ***(Allow 10 minutes.)***

Direct youth to think about the kind of lifestyle they would like to have when they get out on their own. What things do they want to own? What do they consider important? What traditions will they pass on to their family? What new traditions will they begin?

As you ask the following questions, request that the youth think about the answers, but not respond out loud.

➤ **Where will your family fit into your lifestyle?**

➤ **Will this lifestyle be in conflict with God's kingdom?**

➤ **What family traditions will be important to you?**

Have the youth decide what family traditions they want to be more involved with now or want to begin in their family. Ask them to write their thoughts on their YouthPage.

CLOSING CONNECTION

PRAYER TIME

YouthPage, pencils
(Allow 5-7 minutes.)

Have the class pray together the prayer given on the YouthPage. If time allows, the class members could write a prayer for their own family and pray it during a time for personal prayer before reading together the closing prayer.

PRAY:

Heavenly Father, thank you for the families that you have given us. Help us remember the good times we have had with our families and remember the traditions that help make us who we are. Help us to remember we are always growing and changing and we need new traditions, too. May we take advantage of every moment we have together. Let us freely express our love for one another. Amen.

Why All These Family Traditions?

The best thing my family ever did was... ______________________

____

____

____

____

____

T•R•A•D•I•T•I•O•N•S

A tradition is a belief or practice that is handed down to the next generation. Traditions are often repeated or practiced or celebrated yearly. What tradition does your family have for Christmas, Easter, Mother's Day, Father's Day, Independence Day and any other special days? List some of your family traditions in the chart below and then write what your family does and how you are involved.

Example:
Christmas, we decorate a tree, I put on the lights and help with the other decorations.

Tradition	My Family Does	I Do
______	______	______
______	______	______
______	______	______
______	______	______
______	______	______

Jesus' Family Tradition

At the age of twelve, Jesus traveled with his parents to Jerusalem to celebrate Passover. He went to hang out at the Temple while they were visiting. He got so absorbed in discussions about God, he lost all track of time. That may be why retreats are so important to us. As we lose all track of time and let go of our regular schedule, we become open to experiencing our faith in God in a stronger way.

As we lose all track of time and let go of our regular schedule, we become open to experiencing our faith in God in a stronger way.

Jesus' parents didn't know where to find him for three days. Can you imagine what your parents would do if they lost you for three days? This is one time when the family tradition of going to Jerusalem for the Passover celebration did not work out just exactly as Mary and Joseph had planned. But this event does help us learn that as Jesus went from childhood to adulthood, he wanted to learn about spiritual things. Do you think that true maturity is when we want to learn more about God and seek to make God's presence more important to our everyday life? A good family tradition helps us grow in a meaningful way and remember what is important about our family and hopefully our faith.

Do you think that true maturity is when we want to learn more about God and seek to make God's presence more important to our everyday life?

Prayer For My Family

Heavenly Father, thank you for my family. Help us to remember the good times we have had and the traditions that help make us who we are. Help us to remember that we are always growing and changing and we need new traditions, too. May we take advantage of every moment we have together, and let us freely express our love for one another. **Amen.**

SESSION 3:

FAMILY OF GOD

FOCUS

To understand that wherever you go and whatever you do, you are still part of God's family.

SCRIPTURE

Ephesians 3:14-19

HERE'S THE PLAN | DO IT YOUR WAY

OPTIONS	TIME (minutes)	PREPARATION	SUPPLIES
INITIAL CONNECTION			
Create an Acrostic From "God's Family"	10	secure supplies; practice making acrostics before class	large piece of paper, marker and tape or chalk and board
CONNECT WITH THE SESSION			
A Living Stones	12	secure supplies & practice the activity; make copies of YouthPage	building blocks or bricks, a church model, sculpture, or even a picture hidden in a bag or box, table, YouthPages, pencils
B Family of God	10	secure supplies before class	large piece of paper for each small group, crayons
CONNECT WITH THE BIBLE AND THE FAITH COMMUNITY			
Family Chores	12	secure supplies before class	Bibles for the groups, large piece of paper taped to the wall, marker
CONNECT WITH LIFE			
A Only Visiting	10	make copies of YouthPage	YouthPage
B Living in the Family and in the World	10	make copies of YouthPage	Youthpage, pencils
C Family of Living Stones	10	secure supplies	Bibles, large piece of paper, marker, tape
CLOSING CONNECTION			
Prayer Time	5		YouthPage

INITIAL CONNECTION

CREATE AN ACROSTIC FROM "GOD'S FAMILY"

Desired Result:
To begin thinking about what it means to be a part of God's family.

large piece of paper, marker and tape or chalk and board
(Allow 10 minutes.)

Ask the class members if they know what an acrostic is. When a series of words, lines, or verses are represented by the first, last or another letter, the resulting word or phrase is an acrostic or anagram. (Examples: scuba=self-contained underwater breathing apparatus; radar=radio detecting and ranging)

Ask youth to fill in words that describe what God's Family is like. Do this activity on the board or on a large sheet of newsprint. Ask youth to provide several possible words for each letter. Try to make the acrostic into a meaningful phrase they can remember (although making the acrostic into a phrase or sentence is not essential).

CONNECT WITH THE SESSION

A LIVING STONES

Desired Result:
To explore what it means to be part of the family of God.
(Choose Option A or B.)

building blocks or bricks, a church model, sculpture, or even a picture hidden in a bag or box, table, YouthPages, pencils
(Allow 12 minutes.)

As you read the following information, begin stacking building blocks or bricks on the table in front of you. When the stack is high enough, place the church behind the wall. As you begin talking about going out into the world, take the blocks away and tell the class that is what the church or family of God does. We worship together, to find the courage, to bring others into the church, to also become a part of the family of God, by knowing Jesus.

SAY:

- **So, when was the last time you saw a building that was made of stone come to life? What do you think Peter would want you to think about when you read about "living stone" and the other images in this Scripture? "Come to him, a living stone, though rejected by mortals yet chosen and precious in God's sight, and like living stones, let yourselves be built into a spiritual house, to be a royal priesthood, to offer spiritual sacrifices acceptable to God through Jesus Christ." and "Once you were not a people, but now you are God's people" (1 Peter 2:4-5, 10a).**

- **We are a separate family from the world, a community of believers. But God did not call us to stay in a closed group that remains isolated from the world. God's people are called to be a "royal priesthood, a holy**

nation, God's own people," in order to "proclaim the mighty acts" of a God who called his people out of darkness and into the life-giving light. There is a responsibility and a hope with which Christians reach out to others with the invitation to become part of God's people.

Have the youth write in their own words in that space on their YouthPage what it means to be a living stone. Ask for volunteers to tell what they wrote.

large piece of paper for each small group, crayons ***(Allow 10 minutes.)***

B FAMILY OF GOD

Let the class divide into small groups, and give each group a large piece of paper. The groups are to write words, phrases, poems, or draw pictures to illustrate what it means to be a part of the family of God. If there are no large pieces of paper available, groups may tape several pages together to make a poster. Let the groups present and explain their posters.

CONNECT WITH THE BIBLE AND THE FAITH COMMUNITY

Desired Result:
To find out what the Bible has to say about being part of the family of God.

Bibles for the groups, large piece of paper taped to the wall, marker ***(Allow 12 minutes.)***

FAMILY CHORES?

Divide the class into small groups, or let them choose a partner. Assign one of the following passages to each group or pair. Ask the groups to determine what the Scripture says about being part of the family of God and what responsibilities we, as Christians, might have because of this Scripture.

Matthew 28:16-20 (Spread the gospel to all people.)

John 14:1-7 (Jesus is the only true way to God.)

Ephesians 3:14-19 (Families take name and image from God.)

1 Peter 2:4-10 (As living stone we build the family of God.)

1 John 4:7-16 (Live in harmony with one's neighbors.)

Label a large piece of paper with the following column headings: "Family of God" and "Family Responsibilities." As the groups tell what they decided, record the information on the paper.

CONNECT WITH LIFE

Desired Result:
To realize that wherever you go and whatever you do, you are always a part of the family of God.
(Choose Option A, B, or C.)

A. ONLY VISITING

YouthPage
(Allow 10 minutes.)

Ask the youth to slowly read through the questions in their YouthPage and to think about their answers. After giving them time to discuss their answers with a partner, ask them how these questions relate to the Scripture they read earlier.

B. LIVING IN THE FAMILY AND IN THE WORLD

YouthPage, pencils
(Allow 10 minutes.)

Ask the students to do the activity, "Where Do I Fit In?," on their YouthPage. The statements in this activity are intended to spark conversation about the topic. Ask the students to explain their choices and the circumstances when something may be considered to be an activity worthy of a child in the family of God.

Invite the youth to decide upon ways that a godly person can live in our culture and not be overcome by temptations. Christians, even young Christians, are indeed members of a family with a purpose and a destiny. Ask the class members to put into their own words what their purpose and destiny might be.

C. FAMILY OF LIVING STONES

Bibles, large piece of paper, marker, and tape
(Allow 10 minutes.)

Ask the students to decide the responsibilities and privileges of being "living stones" in the family of God. Write their responses on a large piece of paper taped to the wall.

Ask the students to discuss the situations or experiences in their own lives that relate to being a "living stone." This activity asks the students to explore the passage for the deeper meaning of being a "living stone" and a link to the living church. The intent is to help them connect this image to their everyday life.

YouthPage

CLOSING CONNECTION

SAY:

➤ **Jesus is the cornerstone, the most important living stone in the foundation of the family of God. The cornerstone is also what holds the corners of a building together. It is a real linking stone. Jesus' followers are the living stones upon which the church is built and linked together around the world and throughout time into a family. Even on the days that the world rejects us, God loves us enough to keep us as a child in the family of God!**

Invite the class members to stand and read together the closing prayer in the YouthPage. An alternate closing would be to say together the Apostles' Creed given on page 15, as a symbol of beliefs which link together the members of the family of God.

Pray together the following prayer.

Lord, help me to not conform to this world's ways, but to be transformed into a loving and courageous member of the family of God. Amen.

What does it mean
to be a living stone in God's church?

____

____

____

____

CHRISTIANS ARE A DIFFERENT KIND OF FAMILY

As Christians, we have a different set of values from many other people in the world. These values set us apart from the crowd. We seem different because we value truth over slander, generosity over selfishness, sincerity over guile, and love over hatred. But we are not alone. We are a part of a body of believers who have the same values. Christ was rejected by the world, but he became the cornerstone, "very head of the corner." Just as the cornerstone of a building is the piece that connects all the others together and gives definition, so too, does Jesus do that for our lives. We have a community to which we belong, a fellowship of believers. Through Christ, we become the family of God.

WE SEEM DIFFERENT BECAUSE WE VALUE TRUTH OVER SLANDER, GENEROSITY OVER SELFISHNESS, SINCERITY OVER GUILE, AND LOVE OVER HATRED.

I AM ONLY VISITING THIS PLACE.

It is not easy to live in the world as one of God's family without being swept away by the flood of temptations. Although you are in a sense only visiting this place, what you do in your everyday life also matters to God.

Turn to a partner and discuss the following questions. Try to answer with the first thing that comes to mind.

1. Do you ever feel like an alien?
2. Do you stick out or blend into the crowd?
3. Do people at school think you're weird?
4. Do you gossip with the rest of the school when someone gets into trouble?
5. Do you keep your Christianity a secret?
6. Are your friends part of the family of believers?
7. How are you influencing your non-Christian friends?
8. As one of God's family, what responsibilities do you have to help your friends find hope in times of trouble?

WHERE DO I FIT IN?

Is your hope for your future tied to the promises that you see in the media or culture of this world? Or is your hope based upon being a child in God's family and trusting God to help you find your place in this world and the one to come?

Look at the list of situations below and circle the number of the ones that identify the actions of the people of God. Then tell how the Scripture you read earlier might relate to each situation.

Think about the following practices during the coming week.

1. **Cheering for a football team**
2. **Praying for a new car**
3. **Gossiping about a friend who is in trouble**
4. **Talking to a friend who is in trouble**
5. **Skipping band practice to go to church**
6. **Telling a friend to get a life**
7. **Telling a friend how to get a life**

HOW DOES THE SCRIPTURE RELATE TO YOUR OWN LIFE?

What would you need to do differently to follow the directions of the Scripture lesson for today?

Prayer:

Lord, help me to not conform to this world's ways, but to be transformed into a loving and courageous member of the family of God. Amen.

DISCOVERING OUR GIFTS

© JIM WHITMER

SESSION 1: DEFINING THE ISSUES: WHAT'S A GIFT, AND WHO'S THE GIVER?

SESSION 2: DISCOVERING: WHAT GIFTS DO I POSSESS?

SESSION 3: GIFT-GIVING: SHARING OUR GIFTS

Purpose

This unit will assist youth in realizing that each person possesses God-given abilities, which can be used or abused. Once these gifts are identified and claimed, youth will begin to discover how their use of these gifts can impact the world.

This Is Not Junk Mail!

IT'S IMPORTANT STUFF FROM YOUR TEENAGER'S SUNDAY MORNING LEADER

© JIM WHITMER

We live in a culture where we learn at a very young age that we must depend on the affirmation and validation of other people to shape our self-worth. As youth enter adolescence, they begin to develop their own identities and value systems, which many times are reflections of the significant people in their lives. Youth find it difficult to believe that they are worthwhile or gifted at anything. During this time, self-esteem is quite vulnerable and is easily shaken. It is important to find ways to empower youth to recognize themselves as gifted individuals loved by God and others and to teach teenagers to love themselves.

This unit will assist youth in realizing that each person possesses God-given abilities that can be used or abused. Once these gifts are identified and claimed, youth will begin to discover how their use of these gifts can impact the world.

TABLE TALK

Pick a Gift. What gifts do you see in your young person? It is so easy as a parent to focus on the areas in which our young people need to improve and to lose sight of the wonderful treasures that lie within everyone. Each day, affirm at least one of the many gifts that you see in your youth. Help them claim their gifts and explore ways that their gifts can be utilized.

Claim Your Gifts. One of the most effective parenting tools is being a role model. Reflect on the gifts you have been given and find ways to show your young people how God uses these gifts in your everyday life. If this is difficult for you, realize that this is what you are doing every day, whether or not you put it into words. Read I Corinthians 12:4-7, and thank God for the gifts within you.

Hallelujah!

IDEAS FOR PEOPLE WHO PLAN WORSHIP

The following ideas can be used for times of worship or celebration during your class session. You may also share these ideas with your pastor, choir director, and worship work area chairperson to help them discover ideas and resources for making worship more youth-friendly.

MUSIC SUGGESTIONS

Many Gifts, One Spirit
The Gift of Love
This Is My Father's World
Help Us Accept Each Other

PRAYERS OF CONFESSION

Creator God, forgive us when we do not acknowledge you and your creative power. Forgive us for abusing the many gifts that you have given to us. Move us to a new sense of appreciation of you and your creation; in Christ's name. **Amen**.

O giving God, you trust us with so many different gifts and so many times we are afraid to claim them and share them with others. Forgive us when we are afraid to risk and share with others. Challenge us this day to open our eyes to the pathways you have prepared for us; in Jesus name we pray. **Amen**.

WORDS OF ASSURANCE

Hear the good news from John 3:16:
"For God so loved the world that he gave his only Son, so that everyone who believes in him may not perish but may have eternal life."
Thanks be to God!

Hear this promise from Philippians 4:13:
"I can do all things through him who strengthens me."

SCRIPTURE SUGGESTION

I Corinthians 12:4-7, 12-27

AFFIRMATIONS OF FAITH

A Modern Affirmation
(Stress the creative power of God.)

Pastor: Where the Spirit of the Lord is, there is the one true church, apostolic and universal, whose holy faith let us now declare:

Pastor and People:
We believe in God the Father,
infinite in wisdom, power, and love,
whose mercy is over all his works,
and whose will is ever directed to his children's good.

We believe in Jesus Christ,
Son of God and Son of man,
the gift of the Father's unfailing grace,
the ground of our hope,
and the promise of our deliverance from sin and death.

We believe in the Holy Spirit
as the divine presence in our lives,
whereby we are kept in perpetual remembrance
of the truth of Christ,
and find strength and help in time of need.

We believe that this faith should manifest itself
in the service of love
as set forth in the example of our blessed Lord,
to the end that the kingdom of God may come upon the earth. Amen.

SERMON ILLUSTRATIONS

There is a story of a man taking a walk on the beach and encountering a young boy who methodically stooped over, picked up something, and tossed it into the ocean. As the man neared, he could tell that the boy was picking up starfish that had washed ashore and were nearing death from being out of the ocean. The man could see that the shoreline was dotted with hundreds of starfish that had been washed ashore.

The man called to the boy, "Why are you wasting your time? There are so many starfish washed up on the beach, what difference could your efforts make?"

The boy didn't stop his work. He picked up another starfish and tossed it back as he said to the man, "It will make a difference to this one."

God cares about each one of us. God is the life-giver and the gift-giver. Our greatest gift is life. For that we are thankful.

I have heard a story concerning Michelangelo. When questioned by peers concerning why he carefully transported each slab of marble with such precision and care to his workshop, he replied, "Within each piece of stone, there is an angel waiting to be set free."

Within each of us there is an angel waiting to be set free. God has planted within each of us gifts that are special and unique. We are called to identify our gifts and the gifts of others.

Miscellany

IDEAS FOR TEACHERS

WHEN ALL THE YOUTH ARE IN ONE CLASS

The ability to participate in times of self-discovery and personal reflection varies among individuals based on their level of maturity and life experience. Typically, younger adolescents have not spent a great deal of energy wrestling with these issues while older youth have begun to search for their identity whether they articulate this or not. This unit can begin to provide a foundation for the younger youth as well as direction and focus for older youth.

As you divide the class into small groups for various activities, be sure that some senior high youths are in each group in order to provide leadership and direction. Since the older youth will be able to be more self-reflective, this will assist the younger youth in their understanding of their own gifts and how these impact God's plans for their lives.

© JIM WHITMER

It will be very important in a multi-age class to work in small groups so that all members of the class will feel comfortable enough to share their questions and ideas. In the beginning, it may help if you share first in an effort to set the tone of the sharing time. In a large group, the younger youth may be intimidated by the older youth unless a sense of community is established.

IN THE BEGINNING, IT MAY HELP IF YOU SHARE FIRST IN AN EFFORT TO SET THE TONE OF THE SHARING TIME.

SESSION 1:

DEFINING THE ISSUES: WHAT'S A GIFT AND WHO'S THE GIVER?

FOCUS

Each person is an unique individual created and loved by God.

SCRIPTURE

1 Corinthians 12

HERE'S THE PLAN | **DO IT YOUR WAY**

OPTIONS	TIME (minutes)	PREPARATION	SUPPLIES
INITIAL CONNECTION			
A Share Memories	12-15		chalk and chalkboard or newsprint and marker
B Present or Gift?	10-12	make copies of YouthPage	chalk and chalkboard or newsprint and marker, Youth Page, pencils
CONNECT WITH THE SESSION			
A Listing Gift-Bearers	15-18	make copies of YouthPage	YouthPage, pencils, chalk and chalkboard or newsprint and marker
B Brainstorm Important Gifts	15-18		chalkboard and chalk or newsprint and markers
CONNECT WITH THE BIBLE AND FAITH COMMUNITY			
A Scripture Focus	8-10		Bible
B Gifts for God	8-10		Bible
CONNECT WITH LIFE			
B Pass the Gift	10-15	wrap package in white or light paper	wrapped package
CLOSING CONNECTION			
A Group Prayer	1-2	browse through hymnal for unique gifts	

INITIAL CONNECTION

SHARE MEMORIES

Have youth tell about the worst present they have ever received. Ask them to give reasons why they feel this way, and list the reasons for all to see.

Next, have youth tell about one of the best presents they ever received. Again, ask them to give reasons for their responses. List reasons for all to see.

Talk about the word *present*. Have youth define the word. State that a present is often something material given for a specific reason or occasion.

Have youth define the word *gift*. Introduce the concept that a gift is something given with no strings attached, often given for no particular reason.

PRESENT OR GIFT?

Write the word *present* for all to see. Have youth define the word. State that a present is often something material given for a specific reason or occasion.

Write the word *gift* for all to see. Have youth define the word. State that a *gift* is something given with no strings attached, often given for no particular reason.

Complete the "Gift or Present?" list from the Youth Page, keeping in mind the definitions agreed upon by the group.

Invite the total group to discuss their responses.

Desired Result:
To contrast the concepts of "present" and "gift."
(Choose Option A or B.)

chalk and chalkboard or newsprint and marker
(Allow 12-15 minutes.)

chalk and chalkboard or newsprint and marker, YouthPage, pencils
(Allow 10-12 minutes.)

CONNECT WITH THE SESSION

LISTING GIFT-BEARERS

In groups, complete the "Gift-Bearers" activity from the Youth Page. (Note that their list might include people such as the following: pastor, church secretary, school teacher, coach, parent, best friend, youth group leader, custodian.)

Continuing in groups, have youth list the primary gift they believe this person possesses. List the gifts for all to see as the students discuss the activity. Ask the students to decide upon the five gifts they think are the most important.

Desired Result:
To identify gifts seen in the lives of others.
(Choose Option A or B.)

YouthPage, pencils, chalkboard and chalk or newsprint and marker
(Allow 15-18 minutes.)

chalkboard and chalk or newsprint and marker
(Allow 15-18 minutes.)

BRAINSTORM IMPORTANT GIFTS

As a large group, brainstorm ten gifts the youth think are important to have. Have the group rank the gifts in order from most to least important. Come to a group consensus on the value placed upon each gift.

CONNECT WITH THE BIBLE AND THE FAITH COMMUNITY

Desired Result:
Introduce Scripture concerning the importance of all gifts.
(Choose Option A or B.)

Bible
(Allow 8-10 minutes.)

SCRIPTURE FOCUS

Read 1 Corinthians 12:4-7. Have the group restate these verses in their own words. State that any gift possessed by any person is important and can be used by us and by God through us.

Looking back over the list of gifts, have each youth think about which gift they would like to possess. Ask each youth to share with the total group, stating reasons for their choice, as well as stating one way that this gift might be utilized.

Bible
(Allow 8-10 minutes.)

GIFTS FOR GOD

Read 1 Corinthians 12:4-7. Have the group restate these verses in their own words. State that every gift possessed by any person is important and can be used by us and by God through us.

Looking back over the list of gifts from the previous activity, have the group list ways each gift could be used for God.

CONNECT WITH LIFE

PASS THE Gift

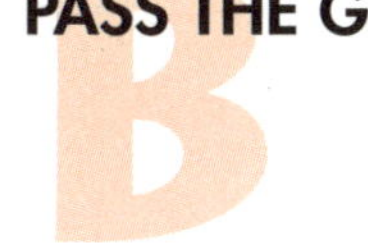

Package wrapped in white or light paper, pens or pencils ***(Allow 10-15 minutes.)***

Gather the group and pass around a wrapped package. As the package is passed to each person, have him or her name the gift that they believe is the most important, or most useful, for them personally. Also, have each youth note this gift on the wrapped package and write a way that they will use this special gift during the coming week. After each person names a gift, have the group respond with the words, "Thank you, God, for the gift of ______________________________ ." Move from this activity to the closing.

CLOSING CONNECTION

GROUP PRAYER

Desired Result:
To remind the group of the variety of gifts given by God.

(Allow 1-2 minutes.)

Ahead of time, you might want to browse through a hymnal for a variety of gifts from God. Many hymns offer beautiful phrasing and unique images to stimulate thinking about God's goodness to us personally and universally.

Close with a prayer of thanksgiving for the gifts exhibited by others, the group of students, and the glorious gifts from God.

Read Me

THIS IS WHAT YOU NEED TO KNOW ABOUT THE TOPIC.

KEY IDEAS IN THIS SESSION

We live in a society where the focus is always on the gifts and talents of someone else. It is easy to focus on others' talents and abilities, which we do not possess, and lose sight of the wonderful gifts within ourselves. Adolescents live in a very egocentric world where their own personal identity is being shaped and where being accepted by others is very important.

It is essential for youth to begin to accept and love themselves without trying to be someone else. Our identity needs to be shaped from within rather than from the perceptions of others. If we can celebrate the fact that we are children of God, created in God's image, with a variety of gifts, we can begin to be all that God has intended us to be.

TEACHER SUGGESTIONS

Read 1 Corinthians 12, as you begin to prepare for this session. What gifts are you willing to use as you lead this class? What gifts will you utilize this week as you live your life? Are there gifts within you that you have not yet discovered?

Prayer

Dear God, thanks for the gifts that you have given me. Help me as I lead others to discover the gifts you have given to each of them. Together, may we discover new ways to share our gifts with others and with you. Amen.

SCRIPTURAL BACKGROUND

Paul's letters to the church in Corinth give instructions and guidelines for living the Christian faith. In the early days of the church, it was important to understand that everyone had a part in the growth and development of the faith; and, every role was vital to its success. In the twelfth chapter of his first letter, to Corinthians Paul is trying to explain that everyone has been given gifts and that each gift is important. Even though the gifts are different, one is not better than another.

GIFT OR PRESENT?

Consider the items listed below.
Indicate whether you believe each item is a gift or a present.

- *Rollerblades*
- *Note from a good friend*
- *Bible*
- *Compact disc*
- *Two hours of babysitting*
- *Telephone (a private line)*
- *Gift certificate*
- *Ability to play the guitar*
- *An extended curfew*

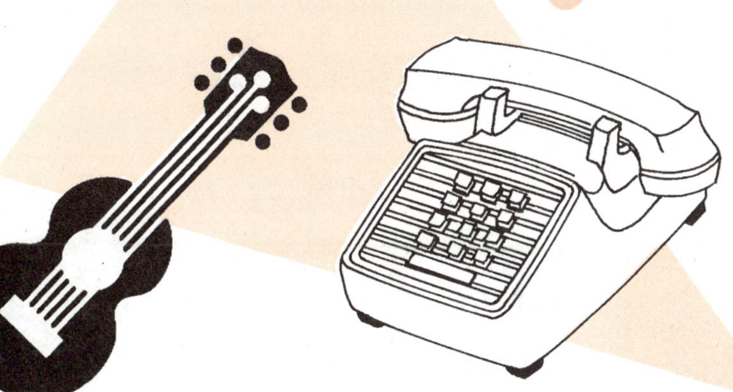

GIFT-BEARERS GIFT-BEARERS

List eight to ten people who make a difference in life. Think about what their gift might be. In other words, how is it that they make a difference?

1. ______________________ 6. ______________________

2. ______________________ 7. ______________________

3. ______________________ 8. ______________________

4. ______________________ 9. ______________________

5. ______________________ 10. ______________________

SESSION 2:

DISCOVERING: WHAT GIFTS DO I POSSESS?

FOCUS

To explore the many gifts each person possesses and to recognize that our differences are also a gift.

SCRIPTURE

1 Corinthians 12:12-27

HERE'S THE PLAN | **DO IT YOUR WAY**

OPTIONS	TIME (minutes)	PREPARATION	SUPPLIES
INITIAL CONNECTION			
Different Gifts	10	shop for different fruits or vegetables	prepared food, paper plates, napkins, or paper towels
CONNECT WITH THE SESSION			
A Silhouettes	25-30	obtain supplies	projector or bright lamp, extension cord (possibly), newsprint, pencils, markers, tape
B Gift Checklist	25-30	make copies of YouthPage	YouthPage, pencils
CONNECT WITH THE BIBLE AND THE FAITH COMMUNITY			
A Scripture Says...	6-8		Bible
B Ham It Up	15-20		Bible
CONNECT WITH LIFE			
Ad Campaign	10-15		Bible, paper, pencils
CLOSING CONNECTION			
A Celebration of Gifts	1-2	make copies of YouthPage	YouthPage
B Closing Prayer	2-3		Bible
C Cheering for God	1-2		

INITIAL CONNECTION

DIFFERENT GIFTS

Ahead of time, gather several different kinds of fruits, or vegetables, cut them into bite-sized pieces, and have them ready to serve to the youth. As the youth gather, have them sample one bite of every fruit and discuss among themselves how the fruits are different. After everyone has sampled the fruits, ask how the fruits are different. After a couple of minutes, ask if it really matters that the fruits are different. **ASK:**

➤ **If all fruits were the same color and texture, wouldn't they be dull?**

➤ **Don't all fruits provide nourishment?**

➤ **Do you think one fruit is more valuable than another?**

➤ **Do you realize that different fruits are different because of the conditions they grow in?**

Desired Result:
To think about how things can be very different, yet have the same value.

prepared fruits or vegetables, small paper plates, napkins or paper towels
(Allow 10 minutes.)

CONNECT WITH THE SESSION

SILHOUETTES

A

As the youths enter, form pairs. Have each pair create silhouettes of each other by having one partner sit in front of a projector or bright light, thus projecting his or her profile upon a sheet of paper taped to the wall. Have the other partner outline the projected profile. Switch places and create the other person's profile. Have youth outline the profile with markers and put their name on the page with the silhouette.

Instruct youth to list the qualities about themselves that they admire within the outline of the silhouette. After a few moments, have youth visit the silhouettes of all other youth in the group, listing qualities that they admire on the outside of each person's silhouette. Stress that only positive attributes are to be listed.

When they have had a chance to visit everyone else's silhouette, call time. Return the silhouettes to the owners and allow them time to look over the comments.

Gather the group together and **ASK:**

➤ **Were you surprised by what others wrote? Why or why not?**

➤ **Was it easier to think of positive qualities about yourself or about others? Why?**

Desired Result:
To identify gifts (positive qualities) in ourselves and others.
(Choose Option A or B.)

projector or bright lamp, extension cord (possibly), newsprint, pencils, markers, tape
(Allow 25-30 minutes.)

State that each of us is special with special gifts, even though we might not always recognize these gifts within ourselves.

YouthPage, pencils
(Allow 25-30 minutes.)

GIFT CHECKLIST

B

Have youth complete the "Gift Checklist" from the YouthPage. Ask the students to turn their sheet over and write their name on the back of the page. Then, gather all youth into a circle. Have the youth pass their page one person to the right, and have each person write a one or two word affirmation about that person. Pass the sheets again. Continue passing sheets until each youth has his or her own page. Allow time for youth to read what others have written.

ASK:

➤ **Were you surprised by what others wrote? Why or why not?**

➤ **Was it easier to identify gifts in others or in yourself? Why?**

CONNECT WITH THE BIBLE AND THE FAITH COMMUNITY

Desired Result:
To examine the Scripture.
(Choose Option A or B.)

SCRIPTURE SAYS...

Bible
(Allow 6-8 minutes.)

Read aloud 1 Corinthians 12:12-27. Have the group discuss in depth what this passage means and what it has to say concerning the previous activities you did, Silhouettes or Gift Checklist.

Bible
(Allow 15-20 minutes.)

HAM IT UP

B

Read 1 Corinthians 12:12-27. Have the group discuss what this passage means and what it has to say concerning the previous activities you did, Silhouettes or Gift Checklist.

Form small groups. Have each group come up with a short skit demonstrating the meaning of the passage, and ask the students to present their skit to the class.

CONNECT WITH LIFE

AD CAMPAIGN

Pass out Bibles and ask the youth to silently read 1 Corinthians 12:12-27.

Get into small groups. Have each group come up with a bumper sticker or slogan to summarize the meaning of the Scripture. (Examples: ONE GOD — BUT MANY GIFTS; NO MATTER WHAT GENDER, RACE, OR RELIGION — WE'RE ALL IN THIS TOGETHER)

Share with the total group. Post these around the room. Encourage the students to duplicate their favorites slogans and put them on their school locker, their notebook, and room at home.

Desired Result:
To encourage the youth to take the day's lesson back to the secular world and to deepen their appreciation for differences of others.

Bible, paper, pencils
(Allow 10-15 minutes.)

CLOSING CONNECTION

Desired Result:
To affirm that God is the giver of our gifts.
(Choose Option A, B, or C.)

CELEBRATION OF GIFTS

A

Gather the group. Together, read "A Celebration of Gifts" from the YouthPage.

YouthPage
(Allow 1-2 minutes.)

CLOSING PRAYER

B

Have youth join hands. Read 1 Corinthians 12:27. Close with prayer thanking God for each person in the group and all of their special gifts.

Bible
(Allow 2-3 minutes.)

CHEERING FOR GOD

C

Gather group together. Have the group repeat each phrase after you in a loud cheerleader-type voice:

> I am special.
> You are special.
> All God's children are special.
> God don't make junk!
> Yea, God!

(Allow 1-2 minutes.)

Read Me

THIS IS WHAT YOU NEED TO KNOW ABOUT THE TOPIC.

YOUTH · NEED HELP · IN DISCOVERING THAT · THEY · ARE UNIQUE CREATIONS · OF GOD · WITH SPECIAL · ABILITIES AND · GIFTS.

© JIM WHITMER

REMEMBER · THAT · YOUNG TEENS · THRIVE · UPON · ACTIVITY.

KEY · IDEAS · IN · THIS · SESSION

Although younger youth often appear cocky and self-confident to others, this outward appearance is many times a mask disguising a fragile ego. Youth want to be loved and accepted for who they are, but who is that? Youth need help in discovering that they are unique creations of God with special abilities and gifts. They need help in identifying these gifts within themselves and affirming the gifts of others.

SCRIPTURAL · BACKGROUND

The Scriptural basis for this session is a continuation of the twelfth chapter of Corinthians, which was used in the previous session. In this passage, Paul addresses the Christians at Corinth, who exist in the midst of a pagan society where almost "everything goes." Paul encourages the Corinthians to celebrate the unique gifts of every person and to join together to build up the church so that it might survive and thrive.

TEACHER · SUGGESTIONS

The teacher should note that this session is based heavily upon interactive exercises. While this concept might initially overwhelm you, remember that young teens thrive upon activity. This lesson will be a distinct break from the read and learn concept often used in class—give it a chance. The youth will remember this one!

Prayer:

Dear Lord, help me to see the youth with whom I work as special and gifted by you. Open us all to new lessons and challenges which might lead to a clearer understanding of ourselves, of others, and of you. Amen.

Gift Check List

Look over the list below. Put a "plus" (+) sign by the qualities you believe that you possess. Then, circle the three qualities you possess that you believe to be the most important.

+++++ooooooooo+++++ooooooooo

•Sense of humor •Musical talent •Acting

•Good listener •Trustworthy •Honest

•Artistic •Athletic •Easy-going •Loyal

•Friendly •Supportive •Easy to talk to

•Kind •Understanding •Positive attitude

•Accepting of others

•Others:______________________

A Celebration of Gifts

God is my Creator. God made me and has given me special gifts. Thank you, God, for all you have given me. Help me to see myself as a special gift from You. Amen.

SESSION 3:

GIFT-GIVING: SHARING OUR GIFTS

FOCUS

To further emphasize how all people are different from one another, but all are valuable and equal in God's sight.

SCRIPTURE

1 Corinthians 12:12-31

HERE'S THE PLAN | DO IT YOUR WAY

OPTIONS	TIME (minutes)	PREPARATION	SUPPLIES
INITIAL CONNECTION			
A Pair Predicaments	12-15		paper, Bibles
B All Tied Up	12-15		rope or cord
CONNECT WITH THE SESSION			
A Scripture Focus	5-7		Bibles
B Scripture Puzzle	5-7	copy 1 Corinthians 12:12-31 on posterboard	paper, pencil or marker, scissors, Bible
C The Most Important Words	5-7		Bible, chalkboard and chalk, or newsprint and marker
CONNECT WITH THE BIBLE AND THE FAITH COMMUNITY			
A Five-Word Skits	15-18		Bibles
B Bag Dramas	15-18	pack enough bags for several groups	bag containing seven to ten items for each group of four youth, Bible
CONNECT WITH LIFE			
Who Were Those Guys?	15-18		paper, pencils, Bible
CLOSING CONNECTION			
A The Body of Christ	6-8		newsprint or poster board, marker
B Community Web	4-6	get supplies ahead of time	yarn, string or rope
C Group Hug	2-3	make copies of YouthPage	YouthPage

INITIAL CONNECTIONS

PAIR PREDICAMENTS

A

Desired Result:
To work as pairs.
(Choose Option A or B.)

paper, Bibles
(Allow 12-15 minutes.)

As youth enter, have them form pairs. Have each pair lock arms and perform tasks with their remaining free arms. You might want to use the following:

> Taking off and putting on each others shoes.
> Carrying a chair from one side of the room to the other side.
> Making a paper airplane and flying it across the room.
> Looking up Matthew 25:14-30.

Call time and gather the group. **ASK:**

➤ **What was difficult about this activity? What was easy?**

➤ **What might have made this activity easier?**

➤ **How might this activity be like everyday living?**

ALL TIED UP

B

rope or cord
(Allow 12-15 minutes.)

As youth enter, form pairs. Tie the wrist of one person with the wrist of another. Then, play a game such as "The Leader Says." Possible tasks might be the following:

> Pat your head.
> Touch your toes.
> Do five jumping jacks.
> Pat your partner on the back.
> Scratch your partner's nose.

ASK:

➤ **What was hard about this activity? What was easy?**

➤ **What might have made this activity easier?**

➤ **How might this activity be like everyday living?**

CONNECT WITH THE SESSION

Desired Result:
Examine the Scripture.
(Choose Option A, B, or C.)

Bibles
(Allow 5-7 minutes.)

SCRIPTURE FOCUS

Read 1 Corinthians 12:12-31 as a large group. Come to group consensus concerning the meaning of the passage.

paper, pencil or marker, scissors, Bible
(Allow 5-7 minutes.)

SCRIPTURE PUZZLE

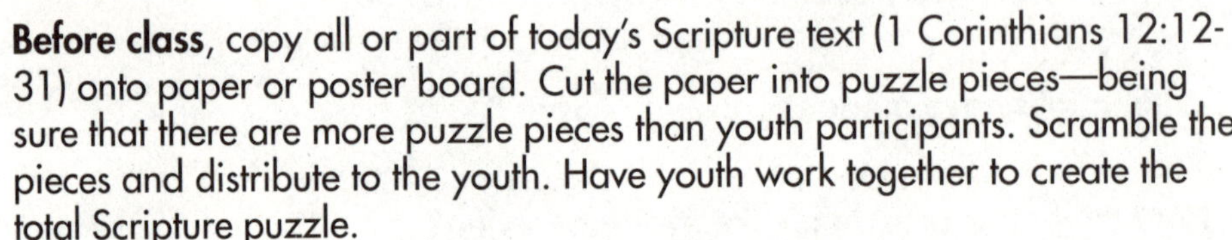

Before class, copy all or part of today's Scripture text (1 Corinthians 12:12-31) onto paper or poster board. Cut the paper into puzzle pieces—being sure that there are more puzzle pieces than youth participants. Scramble the pieces and distribute to the youth. Have youth work together to create the total Scripture puzzle.

Read the Scripture aloud. Come to group consensus concerning its meaning.

Bible, chalkboard and chalk or newsprint and marker
(Allow 5-7 minutes.)

THE MOST IMPORTANT WORDS

Read 1 Corinthians 12:12-31. Come to a group consensus concerning the meaning of the passage. As a group, determine what the youth believe to be the five most important words contained in the Scripture passage. List the five words for all to see. (These words can be used in a later activity entitled "Five-Word Skits.")

CONNECT WITH THE BIBLE AND THE FAITH COMMUNITY

Desired Result:
To work as groups to experience the Scripture.
(Choose Option A or B.)

Bibles
(Allow 15-18 minutes.)

FIVE-WORD SKITS

Have partners from the earlier activity join with another pair to form a larger group. Instruct the groups to create a skit dealing with the meaning of the passage. The catch is that each skit must include a predetermined list of five words, and every person in the group must have a part. (Word lists might include these words from the Scripture passage: body, unity, part, gift, God.)

Share skits with the total group. Note similarities and differences contained within each skit. **ASK:**

➤ **How did everyone participate?**

➤ **What was difficult with this activity?**

➤ **What might have made it easier?**

➤ **What might this activity say to us concerning everyday life?**

BAG DRAMAS

bag with seven to ten items in each for every four youth, Bibles
(Allow 15-18 minutes.)

Have partners from the earlier activity join with another pair to form a larger group. Give each group a bag containing seven to ten items. Have each group come up with a skit dealing with the meaning of the Scripture passage. The skit must involve every member of the group and must use each item within the bag. (Items for the bag can be anything found within the home or classroom. You might include the following: plunger, ball, eraser, flowerpot, pot, hat, trash can, stuffed animal.)

Share skits with the total group. Note the similarities and differences contained within each skit. **ASK:**

➤ **How did everyone participate?**

➤ **What was difficult with this activity?**

➤ **What might have made it easier?**

➤ **What might this activity say to us concerning everyday life?**

CONNECT WITH LIFE

Desired Result:
To help youth realize the value of one another.

WHO WERE THOSE GUYS?

paper, pencils, Bible
(Allow 15-18 minutes.)

Give each youth paper and pencil, and instruct them to individually come up with the names of the twelve disciples. After a few minutes, have youth join with their partner from the previous exercise and work together to come up with a list. After a few more minutes, create larger groups and have the new groups agree upon a list of the twelve disciples. Call time. Read the correct list of the twelve disciples (found in Mark 3:16-19). Have each group report how well they did.

ASK:

➤ **Did anyone do better working individually rather than in a group?**

➤ **How did you feel when working by yourself?**

➤ **How did you feel when working as a group?**

➤ **What was easier about working as a group? What was more difficult about working as a group?**

➤ **What might this activity say to us concerning everyday living?**

Read 1 Corinthians 12:12-27. Restate the passage in your own words. **ASK:**

➤ **What might this passage have to say concerning the activity we just did?**

State that everyone is important in the eyes of God, and that God has given special gifts to each of us that God wants us to share with others. Sometimes, others might not appreciate our gifts; but we are still called to share. Remind the group that we are the body of Christ.

CLOSING CONNECTION

Desired Result: To commit to sharing gifts.

A THE BODY OF CHRIST

newsprint, marker
(***Allow 6-8 minutes.***)

On newsprint, outline the body of the smallest member of the group. Tell the group that the outline symbolizes the body of Christ. Have each youth decide which body part they might represent in the body of Christ as seen through this group. For instance, one might be the heart because she offers love and kindness to others. One might be the ear because he is willing to listen. One at a time, have youths write their name on the body part they represent. Have youth share reasons for their choices. Close with a prayer of thanksgiving for each member of the body of Christ.

B COMMUNITY WEB

yarn, string or rope
(***Allow 4-6 minutes.***)

Gather the group in a circle. Holding one end of a ball of string or yarn, the leader is to offer one gift he or she believes they have which can be used to strengthen this body of Christ. While continuing to hold on the string, toss the rest of the ball to another person, who does the same. Continue tossing and sharing until all persons are holding a piece of the web created by the string.

Point out that the web connects each person. If one person lets go of their string, the web will still exist but it will be weaker. So it is with the body of Christ. Thank each youth for participating. Close in prayer.

GROUP HUG

YouthPage
(***Allow 2-3 minutes.***)

Gather the group in a circle. Close by reading "What Good Are Gifts?" from the YouthPage. Enjoy a group hug.

Read Me

THIS IS WHAT YOU NEED TO KNOW ABOUT THE TOPIC.

KEY IDEAS IN THIS SESSION

With many issues and concepts, we become adept at talking about them, exploring every aspect of the subjects, but never moving to the next step of really experiencing them for ourselves. For young people, and adults for that matter, we retain 90% of what we can experience for ourselves. In this session, the youth will have various opportunities to integrate the Scripture into their own lives and begin to claim the gifts God has given them. Then they can begin to identify how their special abilities can be utilized most effectively.

TEACHER SUGGESTIONS

The best way for young people to explore their gifts is by using them. This session lends itself to a great deal of creative interaction. Do not be intimidated by the use of drama and skits. Younger teens love to "act out" life, and these activities will create great group discussion. The time of commitment at the end will be a very important, as well as a very meaningful, experience. Do not skip this time together.

PRAYER

The focus during this session will be on the final verses of I Corinthians 12, with a special emphasis on verses 27 and 31. It is important to emphasize that God challenges every person to choose the "most excellent way" for their life. God gives the gifts, but the person must decide how each gift will be shared. In this text, Paul was encouraging the people of Corinth to dare to be different from the others around them and to stand up for what they believed in a way that would impact their lives and the world forever.

P•R•A•Y•E•R

O God, you are the source of all our gifts. Help me to use the ones you have given me in a way that helps these young people discover their part in your plan in a deeper and more meaningful way. Thank you for all the gifts you have given, and guide us to a more excellent way of living and sharing together. Amen.

WHAT GOOD ARE GIFTS?

God did not call us to succeed,
God called us to serve.

God did not call us to win,
God called us to work.

God did not call us to live long,
God called us to live for Him.

God did not call us to be happy,
God called us to be hopeful.

God did not call us to fame,
God called us to faith.

God did not call us to seek power,
God called us to seek peace.

God did not call us to loot the earth and each other,

God called us to love our earth and each other.[2]

1,2 From *Guide My Feet* by Marian Wright Edelman. ©1995 by Marian Wright Edelman. Reprinted by permission of Beacon Press, Boston, MA. pages 117 & 118.

Gift Contract

This week, I will attempt to use my gifts in this way:_________________

This week, I will attempt to use my gift in the following ways:

With my friends

____

____

With my family

____

____

Thanks God for trusting me with these gifts!

PRAYER

© Skjold Photography

SESSION 1: WHAT IS PRAYER?

SESSION 2: WHAT DOES JESUS TEACH ABOUT PRAYER?

SESSION 3: WHAT DIFFERENCE DOES PRAYER MAKE?

Purpose

To seek definitions of prayer as revealed in the Bible and in the life and teachings of Jesus, and to explore ways the practice of prayer in the Christian tradition make a difference in our lives and in the world.

This Is Not Junk Mail!

IT'S IMPORTANT STUFF FROM YOUR TEENAGER'S SUNDAY MORNING LEADER

Your youth is involved in a unit on prayer. Consider ways your family can be more involved in prayer for the next few weeks in order to strengthen the spiritual growth offered in this unit.

WHAT ARE YOU DOING NOW?

What is your family's prayer life? Do you pray at bedtimes and meals? Do you pray as a family or as individuals or both? What can you do to improve the quality of family prayer?

Your youth will learn that there are many ways to pray, and no one way is right or wrong. Methods of prayer are tools that help a person find relationship with God. True prayer is opening the mind and heart to God's love and grace. It is seeking for communion with God through Christ.

God accepts everyone as they are

If you raised your children with memorized prayers at bedtimes and mealtimes, talk about the prayers. What do they mean? How did your youth feel as they prayed these prayers?

HAVE FAMILY DISCUSSIONS

Invite your youth to talk about their definitions of prayer. Tell your youth your own definition for prayer. What can you learn from one another about prayer?

Discuss what "answered" prayer means. Do you think it means getting exactly what your pray for? How does God answer prayer?

Make a family prayer calendar.

Allow your youth to talk about any negative feelings he or she may have about prayer. Have you had similar feelings? What are they? Why do you think you or your youth have experienced such feelings?

IDEAS FOR FAMILY PRAYER

Family gatherings are popular times for someone to pray aloud. Expand these times for prayer by offering a variety of prayer experiences. You might pray by being silent together. Buy a book of guided imagery prayers based upon Scripture, and invite your family to participate as you lead. Ask family members to make up personal prayers.

INVITE YOUR YOUTH TO PRAY

Make a family prayer calendar. Mark birthdays and special events in the lives of each member of the family on this calendar. You might use photos as reminders. Encourage all family members to pray for the events you have placed on the calendar.

A WORD OF CAUTION

Avoid using a time of prayer to discipline or correct your youth. Help them grow in their understanding of prayer as a time of opening their minds and hearts to God. You can help them more in their spiritual growth by reminding them that God loves them and listens to their prayers. God accepts everyone as they are. God offers forgiveness and grace to all who seek these gifts.

Hallelujah!

IDEAS FOR PEOPLE WHO PLAN WORSHIP

Session 1: Option 3C invites the youth to create an order of worship. Use this as the basis for congregational worship on a Sunday morning.

Session 2: Both Options 3C and 4C use a prayer cube developed from the content of John 17. Pastors, consider using John 17 for a sermon text. Incorporate the activity of creating the Prayer Cube. Adjust the activity to invite the entire congregation to pray for all Christians.

In Option 4B, youth create Lord's Prayer wallpaper. Display the wallpaper in a prominent area. Invite members of the congregation to add sketches to the wallpaper.

Session 3: Option 1B describes a mime of Psalm 150. Option 2A offers a variety of prayer "tools" in a guided imagery prayer. Both of these activities could be easily adapted for use in the Sunday morning worship setting.

Option 4B uses Mark 11:23-24. Why not put an image or sketch of a mountain on the cover of an order of worship and invite congregational worshipers to identify mountains that block them on their Christian journeys?

OTHER IDEAS

A mission/prayer project is suggested in "When all the Youth are in One Class." If you decide to do the project, plan a worship service as a part of the experience.

Have the youth create a prayer chapel that they may use throughout the unit on prayer. An area beneath a stair well makes an excellent place to create a small altar for prayer. You may want to use a closet, which ties in well with Session 2. All you need is a floor pillow, a small table or bench to use for an altar, a candle, and a Bible or other reading material.

Have a prayer vigil. Identify a specific concern or reason for people to pray. Invite them to sign up for specific times. Prepare the sanctuary or a prayer chapel so that people may come in and out to pray at specified times.Have a prayer service in which worshipers can experience a variety of ways to pray. Plan the service to include silent prayer, vocal prayer, litanies, memorized prayers, and so forth.

Miscellany

IDEAS FOR TEACHERS

When All the Youth Are in One Class

Middle school youth are active!

There are many creative adjustments that you can make with the sessions when all the youth in your group meet together.

Developmentally, senior high youth are better able to be still and to reflect upon ideas or questions. There are many creative adjustments that you can make with the sessions when all the youth in your group meet together. Be sensitive to the individual and developmental differences and similarities among your youth. Adjust the activities to meet the needs of your class.

Psalm 150 which is the basis for Session 3, Option1A, provides an excellent opportunity for such adjustments. The option in session 3 is designed to help middle school youth experience that prayer can be both active and loud. You can use this activity to broaden the way both middle school and senior high youth think about prayer. One good idea is to follow this activity with a time of silent listening to God. The movement of the heart would be from joyous praise to quiet listening. You may be surprised at the way your middle school youth can become still and silent! And your senior high youth may get into the activity of miming.

Some senior high youth may, however, feel the need to be "mature," which can inhibit an experience of joyous, active prayer. These youth may not be interested in doing the miming as described in the activity. Adjust the activity from a mime to an enthusiastic reading in the style of a "Scripture choir." Assign lines to individuals and to the entire group and have them do the Psalm as a choral reading.

Tools and True Prayer

Prayer is accomplished in many ways. This unit gives an overview of biblical teachings about prayer. Session 3, "What Difference Does Prayer Make?" touches on the many ways of praying in our Christian tradition and how these ways of praying are tools for true prayer, which is opening the mind and heart to God's love and will through Jesus Christ. The intent and focus of the true prayer leads beyond the form to this opening of heart and mind. True prayer leads to compassion toward our neighbor and to the desire for justice and peace in our world. Both corporate and private prayer make a difference when our daily actions engage and reflect issues of compassion, justice, and peace.

True prayer is opening the mind and heart to God's love and will through Jesus Christ.

Plan a Mission and Prayer Project

T • H • I • N • K

Think about some of the needs in your community. Do you know anyone in a rest home or convalescent center who would be cheered by a visit? Do you have a food drive? What mission outreach project can you organize for the youth? Decide on a project, contact any appropriate agencies, and plan your participation. Combine the project with the discipline of prayer. Pray for the project in class. Make a prayer calendar for the youth to use during the unit on prayer. Close the unit with **DOING** your mission project.

Worship Ideas

P • R • A • Y • E • R

Prayer is always two-fold in that it involves both solitude and community. In other words, we can pray alone or together, and our prayer transforms our individual lives and our communal lives. This unit on prayer affords the entire congregation an opportunity to pray and to reflect upon prayer in their personal lives and in the life of the church. Use some of the ideas on these pages, or develop suggestions from the youth, to involve all the church in prayer as the youth participate in this unit on prayer.

SESSION 1:
WHAT IS PRAYER?

FOCUS

To explore definitions of prayer revealed in the Bible and the faith community.

SCRIPTURE

Genesis 18:22-32; 24:12-14; 32:11; Exodus 3:1-4; 5:22-23; 32:11-13, 31-32; 33:11; Leviticus 16:21; 26:40-45; Numbers 11:11-15; Judges 16:28; 2 Samuel 12:16-17; 24:17; 1 Kings 3:5-14; 8:22-53; Nehemiah 9:16-37; Psalms 31:15; 51; 59:1; 100:4-5; 108:3-4; 137:7; 145-150; Proverbs 30:8; Isaiah 1:18; Jeremiah 17:18; Ezekiel 9:8; Dan 9:20; Amos 7:1-6; Micah 7:18-19; Matthew 6:11; 7:11; Luke 18:13; Acts 1:24-25; 6:6; 7:60; 13:2-3; Romans 1:8-9; 15:13; 30-32; 1 Corinthians 1:4; 2 Corinthians 1:11; Philippians 1:3-5, 9-11; 4:6; 1 Thessalonians 5:25; James 5:13-16.

HERE'S THE PLAN | **DO IT YOUR WAY**

OPTIONS	TIME (minutes)	PREPARATION	SUPPLIES
INITIAL CONNECTION			
A Prayer Pictionary	8		large sheets of newsprint and markers
B Awareness Game	8		
CONNECT WITH THE SESSION			
A Prayer Crossword	8	make copies of YouthPage	YouthPage
B Discuss Prayer as Communication	10	make copies of YouthPage	YouthPage
CONNECT WITH THE BIBLE AND THE FAITH COMMUNITY			
A Re-enact conversation with God	10		chair
B Kinds of Prayer	10	gather supplies	chalkboard and chalk or large white paper and markers, small pieces of paper, basket or bowl, list of Bible passages
C Order of Worship	10	gather supplies	orders of worship from a service in your congregation, paper, pencils, YouthPage
CONNECT WITH LIFE			
A "Home" Poster	12	make copies of YouthPage	Bible, Read Me, YouthPage, poster paper, markers
B "Going Home" Prayer	12	make copies of YouthPage	Bible, Read Me, YouthPage
C "Heart" Prayer	8	make copies of YouthPage; cut out hearts from red construction paper—one for each youth	Bible, Read Me, YouthPage, red paper hearts, pens or pencils
CLOSING CONNECTION			
Worship Together	5		

INITIAL CONNECTION

PLAY PRAYER PICTIONARY

Ask the youth to form two teams. Have one team think of something to pray for and tell this to one member of the opposing team. That member must draw the prayer on a sheet of newsprint for the others on his or her team to guess. The time limit for drawing and guessing is one minute. If the team guesses the prayer from the drawing, they get a point. If they do not guess the prayer, the other team gets a point. The first team to get five points wins.

Desired Result:
To become better acquainted with one another and with popular ideas about prayer.
(Choose Option A or B.)

large sheets of newsprint and markers, timer or a watch with a second hand
(Allow 8 minutes.)

AWARENESS GAME

(Allow 8 minutes.)

Ask the youth to choose partners, and to discuss with their partner their responses to the following open-ended sentences:

- **My name is ______________________________.**
- **My favorite activity is ______________________________.**
- **I think prayer is ______________________________.**

After the partners have talked for about a minute, tell them to stand back-to-back, about a foot apart from each other. Each youth will change three things about his or her appearance. (For example, remove glasses, change hair, put a pen in a shirt pocket, take off jewelry, unbutton or button a shirt, and so on.) When they have done this, have the partners face one another and try to identify the three changes.

ASK:

- **Each day we pass by things that are familiar, but we may not notice them. How many things can you think of in your daily life that you "look" at but do not "see?"**
- **When have you had a similar experience with being aware of God's presence?**

CONNECT WITH THE SESSION

Desired Result:
To explore definitions of prayer.
(Choose Option A or B.)

PRAYER CROSSWORD

A

YouthPage
(Allow 8 minutes.)

Have the youth add words that tell about prayer to the prayer crossword on the YouthPage. Invite the youth to tell about their crosswords.

ASK:

➤ **What do these words say to you about prayer?**

➤ **What is your definition of prayer?**

You may also do this activity as a group by writing the word "prayer" on a chalkboard or large sheet of paper. Youth take turns adding one word to the crossword and telling about the word they add.

PRAYER AS COMMUNICATION

B

YouthPage
(Allow 10 minutes.)

Give each youth a copy of the YouthPage. Read the section entitled "Prayer—Communicating with God." Invite the youth to add other forms of communication to the list. Tell them to fill in the blanks in the sentence.

ASK:

➤ **What form of communication best describes prayer for you? Why?**

Have the youth tell about what they wrote in the sentence on the YouthPage. Read the section entitled "What's in a Prayer?" on the YouthPage. **ASK:**

➤ **For what purpose do you most often pray?**

CONNECT WITH THE BIBLE AND THE FAITH COMMUNITY

Desired Result:
To explore ways people pray in the Bible and in the faith community.
(Choose Option A, B, or C.)

RE-ENACT CONVERSATION WITH GOD

A

chair
(Allow 10 minutes.)

Have a youth read aloud Exodus 33:11.

ASK:

➤ **What do you think it might be like to talk to God face to face?**

Have another youth read Exodus 3:1-4.

ASK:

➤ **What did Moses learn from conversation with God?**

Place a chair in front of the class. Write GOD on a sheet of paper and tape it to the back of the chair. Tell the youth to imagine that God is sitting in the chair.

ASK:

➤ **What do you want to talk about with God? What would you ask God? What do you think God would say to you?**

KINDS OF PRAYER

chalkboard and chalk or large white paper and markers, small pieces of paper, basket or bowl, list of Bible passages
(Allow 10 minutes.)

Write the following categories of prayer on a chalkboard or large sheet of paper:

guidance	**help with needs**	**intercession**
confession	**forgiveness**	**praise & thanksgiving**

Write the following Bible verses on small pieces of paper, one verse to each piece, and place them in a bowl or basket:

Genesis 18:22-32; 24:12-14; 32:11; Exodus 3:1-4; 5:22-23; 32:11-13, 31-32; 33:11; Leviticus 16:21; 26:40-45; Numbers 11:11-15; Judges 16:28; 2 Samuel 12:16-17; 24:17; 1 Kings 3:5-14; 8:22-53; Nehemiah 9:16-37; Psalms 31:15; 51; 59:1; 100:4-5; 108:3-4; 137:7; 145-150; Proverbs 30:8; Isaiah 1:18; Jeremiah 17:18; Ezekiel 9:8; Dan 9:20; Amos 7:1-6; Micah 7:18-19; Matthew 6:11; 7:11; Luke 18:13; Acts 1:24-25; 6:6; 7:60; 13:2-3; Romans 1:8-9; 15:13; 30-32; 1 Corinthians 1:4; 2 Corinthians 1:11; Philippians 1:3-5, 9-11; 4:6; 1 Thessalonians 5:25; James 5:13-16.

Have a youth draw a piece of paper from the basket, find the text in a Bible, and decide which category of prayer the passage illustrates.

ASK:

➤ **Which type of prayer do you pray most often? What can you do to include other kinds of prayer? How do you think this might help you in your growth as a Christian?**

orders of worship from a service in your congregation, paper, pencils, YouthPage
(Allow 10 minutes.)

CREATE AN ORDER OF WORSHIP

Read "What's in a Prayer" on the YouthPage. Give the youth copies of an order of worship from your church's worship service. Use the information on the YouthPage to identify what types of prayer are on your church's order of worship.

Have the youth form teams of three or four. Tell each team to write their own prayers and use them to create an order of worship. When they have finished, have each team read the prayers in their orders of worship.

Invite your pastor to use the prayers created by the youth in your class.

Desired Result:
To experience prayer as "Going Home" to God's safety rest, and nourishment.
(Choose Option A, B, or C.)

Bible, Read Me, YouthPage, poster paper, markers
(Allow 12 minutes.)

"HOME" POSTER

Read aloud John 14:1-3 and the information in "Prayer—Going Home to God's Heart" on the Read Me page. Have a youth read "How Do I Pray?" from the YouthPage.

SAY: For most people home is a place of safety, rest, and nourishment. Home provides food and shelter. Home is the place where we can most be ourselves.

ASK:

- **What place in your life feels most like a place of safety, rest, and nourishment?**

- **What kinds of feelings, thoughts, and images come to your mind when you hear the word "home?"**

Have the youth draw a poster depicting a place of safety and rest that seems like "home." Have them tell about their "home."

ASK:

- **How is prayer like "going home" to God?**

- **How can you "go home" to God during the middle of a busy day at school?**

B "Going Home" Prayer

Bible, Read Me, YouthPage
(Allow 8 minutes.)

Do Option A, but do not make the poster. Simply discuss "home" as a place of safety, rest, and nourishment. Have the youth close their eyes and become very still. Tell them to relax and try to imagine what you read. **Read** the following.

Imagine a place of safety, rest, and nourishment. In this place no one hurts you. Everyone expects that you will just be yourself. Everyone loves you just as you are. Where is this place? Who are the people there? (Pause a moment.)

Imagine that God is with you in this place. God loves you just as you are. God wants you to be safe, to rest, and to have nourishment. What is it like to be with God? (Pause a moment.)

Spend some time talking with God in this place. Listen to what God tells you. Say goodbye. Know that you can return "home" to God anytime you want to. Get a sense of yourself here in the Sunday school class. When you are ready, open your eyes.

Invite any youth who would like to talk about this experience to speak. Remind them again that they can return "home" to God anytime they desire by using God's gift of imagination.

C HEART PRAYER

Bible, Read Me, YouthPage, red construction paper hearts, pens or pencils
(Allow 8 minutes.)

Ahead of time cut out hearts from the red construction paper. Make sure you have enough hearts for all the youth in your class. Do Option A, but do not make the poster. Simply discuss "home" as a place of safety, rest, and nourishment. Tell the youth to imagine that they are going to take a journey "home" to visit with God. Give each youth a heart cutout. Tell them to imagine that they are taking their "heart" home to God. Have them write a prayer on one side of the heart. The prayer should be something they sincerely want to talk to God about. Allow time to write the prayers.

Have the youth close their eyes and pray their "heart" prayers silently. Tell them to pay attention to anything that might seem to come to them from God's heart. After a few moments of silent prayer, have the youth write anything they think God might want them to know or hear on the other side of their prayer hearts.

CLOSING CONNECTION

(*Allow 5 minutes.*)

WORSHIP TOGETHER

Have the youth stand in a prayer circle. Tell them to think of one for whom they would like to pray. Pray the following prayer or one of your own aloud.

God of all people, we pray in so many ways. You hear us. You accept the prayers of our hearts and you take them into your own heart. Hear us now as we name the people we care about. (Ask youth to say the name of the one person for whom they would like to pray.) **We know that you know their needs, God. We know that your will for them is good. We thank you and we praise you; in the love of Christ, we pray. Amen.**

Read Me

THIS IS WHAT YOU NEED TO KNOW ABOUT THE TOPIC.

P•R•E•P•A•R•I•N•G YOURSELF

This session focuses on definitions of prayer. What is your definition of prayer? Read over the material in Bible Background below. Read the Bible passages and YouthPage. What, if anything, would you now add to your definition?

BIBLE BACKGROUND

The book of Exodus describes Moses' communication with God as one to one conversation (Exodus 3:1-4; 33:11). Both Moses' call and directions for leading the people of Israel come from conversations with God. Conversation, sometimes within a dream, also occurs with Adam, Abraham, kings, and prophets throughout the Old Testament.

The word "pray" originally meant to ask or beg earnestly. Today its meaning includes many ways of communicating with God in addition to asking for something. Communication includes such acts as listening, gesturing, being silent, and creating, in addition to conversing.

A survey of prayer in the Bible provides an array of diverse occasions and purposes for prayer.
• Biblical patriarchs, kings, prophets, and disciples pray for guidance (Genesis 24:12-14; Numbers 11:11-15; 1 Kings 3:5-14; Acts 1:24-25; 6:6; 13:2-3).
• They ask for divine help with necessities of life (1 Kings 8:22-53; Proverbs 30:8; Matthew 6:11; 7:11; Philippians 4:6), deliverance from enemies (Genesis 32:11; Psalms 31:15; 59:1), retribution (Judges 16:28; Psalms 137:7; Jeremiah 17:18), and healing (James 5:13-16).
• Intercessions, or prayers for others, are made for both the whole people and for individuals in order that all the people may experience wholeness and peace (Genesis 18:22-32; Exodus 5:22-32; 32:11-13; 2 Samuel 12:16-17; Amos 7:1-6; Ezekiel 9:8; 11:13).

•They are offered for congregations (Romans 15:13; Philippians 1:9-11) and for individuals like Paul (Romans 15:30-32; 2 Corinthians 1:11; 1 Thessalonians 5:25).

Read Me

THIS IS WHAT YOU NEED TO KNOW ABOUT THE TOPIC.

• Prayers of praise and thanksgiving are offered for God's steadfast love (Psalms 100:4-5; 108:3-4), for the creation and care of the world (Psalms 145-150), for faith and witness (Roman 1:8-9; 1 Corinthians 1:4; Philippians 1:3-5), and as general acts of worship (Acts 2:46-47).

• Confession and forgiveness occur on the annual Day of Atonement (Leviticus 16:21) and on behalf of people (Exodus 32:31-32; Nehemiah 9:16-37; Daniel 9:20).

• They are offered by community (Judges 10:10) or by individuals (2 Samuel 24:17; Psalm 51) and are made in certainty of God's promise to forgive (Leviticus 26:40-45; Isaiah 1:18; Micah 7:18-19).

• Forgiveness is requested for the self (Luke 18:13; Matthew 6:12) and for others (Acts 7:60). Prayer may occur at any time or place. The Bible lists prescribed times for the people like the Day of Atonement, the Sabbath, and festival days. Particular hours were set for daily prayer.

• People prayed in the Temple, synagogue, and home. In addition to honoring these traditions, Jesus often retreated into the wilderness to pray. Early Christians met to pray, sing, tell stories about Jesus, and share the Lord's Supper.

• Prayer is attitude and action as well as ritual. It must be offered honestly from the heart and with the intent of attending to ethical concerns (Isaiah 1:15-17; Hosea 6:6; Amos 5:21-24; Micah 6:8; Psalms 24:3-6).

• The overall picture in the Bible is that prayer is to be made to God in faith and expectation, and in the New Testament, through Christ and in the Spirit. Prayer is not done as an attempt to manipulate God but to give God thanks and praise, to ask for help with daily needs, care for self and others, and that God's will be done and God's kingdom come.

Prayer-Going Home To God's Heart

Richard Foster, author of *Prayer: Finding the Heart's True Home*, explores prayer as movement, an active process in which persons move inward to seek transformation, upward to seek needed intimacy, and outward to seek ways to minister to the needs of others. Foster understands these movements as movements toward each person of the Trinity, inward to God the Son in Jesus Christ, upward to God the Father, and outward to God the Holy Spirit. The movements may also be viewed as expressions of the great commandment to love God, love self, and love neighbor. Prayer, the movement toward communion with God, is not separate from communion with self and neighbor. Being alone with God nourishes active involvement with the world.

GRATITUDE
PRAYER
LOVE

PRAYER—WHAT IS IT?

Make a prayer crossword puzzle by adding words across or down that tell about prayer:

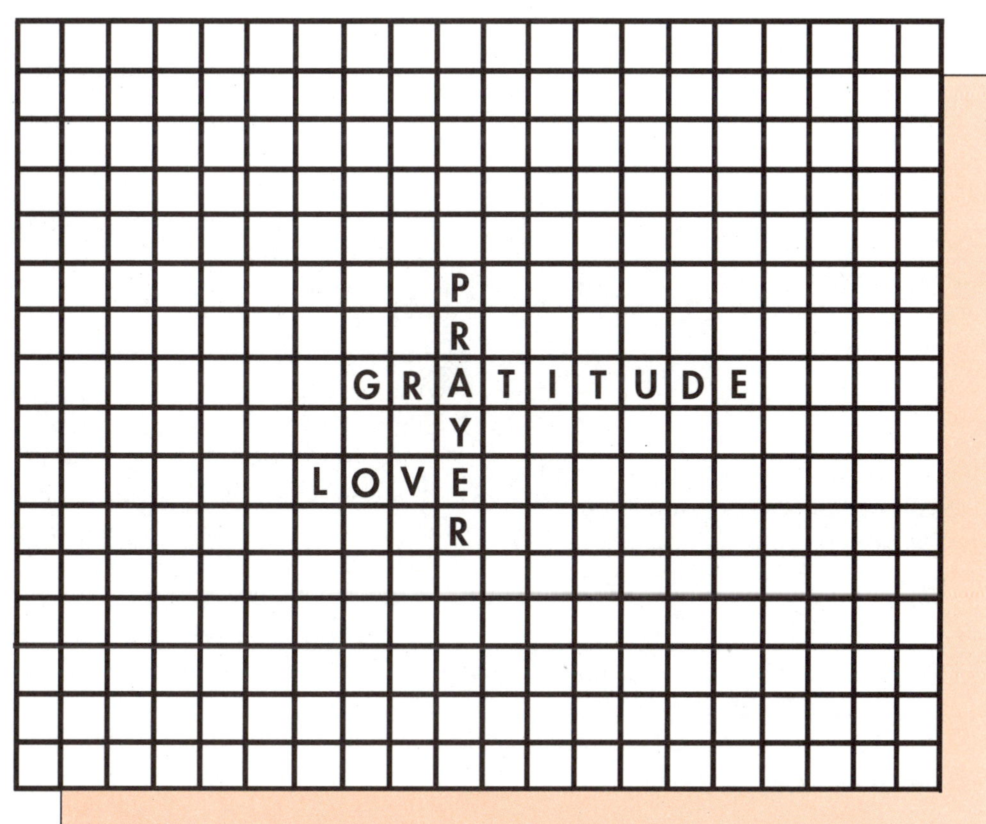

Hey! Copy this page for your youth—really, we want you to!

PRAYER COMMUNICATING WITH GOD

People communicate with one another in many ways. Below is a list of some methods of communication:

- Δ Face To Face Conversation
- Δ Telephone
- Δ E-Mail
- Δ Answering Machines
- Δ Television Movies
- Δ Books
- Δ Audio
- Δ Tapes
- Δ American Sign Language
- Δ Video Tapes
- Δ Dance Music
- Δ Art
- Δ Other?

We can think of prayer as communicating with God, but we cannot see or hear God in the same way that we see or hear other human beings. Look at the methods of communication listed above and fill in the following sentence:

I think prayer is like ______________________,
because ______________________________

____

____

____

WHAT'S IN A PRAYER?

People have reasons for communicating with one another and with God. Prayer has purpose. The church uses some words to describe some of the traditional purposes of prayer.

ADORATION-Praising or loving God

CONFESSION-Telling God our failures

THANKSGIVING-Saying "Thank You" to God

SUPPLICATION-Asking God for something

INTERCESSION-Asking God to help others

INVOCATION-Asking God to be present

BENEDICTION-Asking for God's blessing

HOW DO I PRAY?

People pray alone or in groups, aloud or silently, with or without words.

People create music, dance, and art to show praise for God. Some go into nature to feel closer to God. Others attend worship and participate in liturgies. Some people kneel and others stand. People use Scriptures, candles, statues, smells, pictures, or sounds to help them pay attention to God. All of these methods are tools of prayer. True prayer happens when the heart seeks to be "at home" with God.

SESSION 2

WHAT DOES JESUS TEACH ABOUT PRAYER?

FOCUS

To explore prayer in the life and teachings of Jesus.

SCRIPTURE

Matthew 6; Luke 3:21; 5:15-16; 6:12; 9:29; 11:1-13; 22:39-46; 23:34, 46; John 17:1

HERE'S THE PLAN | DO IT YOUR WAY

OPTIONS	TIME (minutes)	PREPARATION	SUPPLIES
INITIAL CONNECTION			
A Lord's Prayer Relay Race	10	copy Lord's Prayer onto poster	
B Blessing Web	10	make copies of YouthPage	YouthPage, ball of yarn
CONNECT WITH THE SESSION			
A What's In Your Closet?	10	make copies of YouthPage	YouthPage, pencils
B Flowery Prayers	10	make flower poster & copies of YouthPage	YouthPage, paper, pencil, poster paper
CONNECT WITH THE BIBLE AND THE FAITH COMMUNITY			
A Private Eyes	10	make copies of YouthPage	YouthPage
B Gethsemane Prayer	10		Bibles, chalkboard and chalk or large white paper and markers, Read Me
C John 17 Prayer Box	10	YouthPage, Bibles,	a cube cardboard box, white wrapping paper, tape, markers, Bibles
CONNECT WITH LIFE			
A Luke 18:1-8 & Luke 18:9-14 Skits	12		Bible
B Lord's Prayer Wallpaper	10	make copies of YouthPage	roll of white freezer paper or wrapping paper, markers, King James Bible, NRSV Bible, any other translations of the Bible that are available, YouthPage
C Pray for All Christians	5		prayer cube created in activity 3C, small table, Bible, cross, a candle in a candle holder, matches
CLOSING CONNECTION			
Sing a Prayer			hymnal (or other source for "Thy Word is a Lamp")

INITIAL CONNECTION

Desired Result:
To enjoy physical activity and to encounter the theme of prayer.
(Choose Option A or B.)

(Allow 10 minutes.)

LORD'S PRAYER RELAY RACE

NOTE: It might be a good idea to have the Lord's Prayer written out in large letters on a piece of newsprint or posterboard and posted—just in case the youth get nervous or embarrassed and forget the words during the game.

Ask the youth to form two teams, and to then line up. They will run a relay race as follows:

> The first person on each team will run to a designated spot,
> get on his or her knees,
> pray aloud the Lord's Prayer,
> then run back and tag the next person on the team,
> who then repeats the process.

The first team to finish wins.

YouthPage, ball of yarn
(Allow 10 minutes.)

BLESSING WEB

Tell the youth to think of a blessing, table grace, or bedtime prayer they may have heard in childhood or that their family uses at mealtime.

Hold the free end of the yarn. Throw the ball of yarn to a youth. The youth must quickly say a blessing, table grace, or bedtime prayer, hold on to the yarn, and throw the ball of yarn to another youth. He or she in turn must quickly repeat the same process. A Blessing Web will be created as each person, in turn, says a prayer, holds on to the yarn, and throws the ball of yarn to another youth. Have the last youth throw the ball of yarn to you. End this activity by saying your favorite blessing, table grace, or bedtime prayer.

CONNECT WITH THE SESSION

Desired Result:
To explore Jesus' teachings about praying honestly and sincerely to God.
(Choose Option A or B.)

YouthPage, pencils
(Allow 10 minutes.)

WHAT'S IN YOUR CLOSET?

Read Matthew 6:5-6. Have the youth read to themselves "What's in Your Closet?" on the YouthPage, and to respond to the questions in this section.

Ask the youth to write or draw one thing in their closet that they think no one would be able to guess. Have them turn their YouthPage over so no one can see what they have written or drawn. Tell the youth to stand up, go to each person, and try to guess what is in his or her closet within three guesses. When someone guesses what is in a youth's closet, that youth must sit down. The last one standing wins. Tell the youth to imagine that their hearts and minds are closets. **ASK:**

➤ **What thoughts are in your closet? what feelings?**

SAY:

➤ **Going into the "closet" to pray means offering your feelings and thoughts to God. God cares about what you have in your closet.**

FLOWERY PRAYERS

YouthPage, paper, pencil, poster paper
(Allow 10 minutes.)

Ahead of time sketch a large flower on the poster paper. Write the following prayer inside the flower: "God, teach me to love." Place the poster where everyone can see it.

Read aloud Matthew 6:7. Have one youth read aloud the section entitled "K.I.S.S." on the YouthPage. Have the youth form two or three teams. Have each team write a "flowery" prayer by adding lots of empty phrases to the prayer to make it long and showy. Have each team read aloud their flowery prayers.

CONNECT WITH THE BIBLE AND THE FAITH COMMUNITY

Desired Result:
To explore ways Jesus prayed.
(Choose Option A, B, or C.)

PRIVATE EYES

YouthPage, pencils
(Allow 10 minutes.)

Have the youth form two teams. Tell them to pretend that they are private investigators. They have been hired to find out what Jesus did during crucial times in his life. Have each team look up the Scripture passages in "What Did Jesus Do?" on the YouthPage. Each team will look up the Scriptures, identify what was going on in Jesus' life, and what Jesus did. The first team to finish the assignment wins.

Bibles, chalkboard and chalk or large white paper and markers, Read Me
(Allow 10 minutes.)

GETHSEMANE PRAYER

B

Read aloud Luke 22:39-46. Write "Jesus' Prayer Life" and "My Prayer Life" on a chalkboard or large sheet of white paper. Assign each verse of this passage to the youth, one verse to a youth. Have the first youth read verse 39.
ASK:

➤ **What does this verse teach us about Jesus' prayer life?**

➤ **If we want to be like Jesus, what can we do when we pray?**

Write responses beneath the topics on the chalkboard or large white paper.

Have each youth read his or her verse, and repeat the process of asking questions, hearing responses, and writing them beneath the topics. After everyone has read his or her verse, tell the information given in the Bible Background on Read Me about this passage .

cube-shaped cardboard box, white wrapping paper, tape, markers, Bibles
(Allow 10 minutes.

JOHN 17 PRAYER CUBE

C

Have the youth wrap the cardboard box with white paper. Read aloud John 17. Ask the youth to identify what Jesus prayed for. Tell them to write and illustrate these on the box to create a Prayer Cube of John 17. When they have finished, have them tell what they found in Jesus' prayer about the following:

The Son's glory	eternal life
believers	God's protection
joy	God's word
unity	God's love

Use this prayer cube in activity 4C, on the next page.

CONNECT WITH LIFE

A LUKE 18:1-8 AND LUKE 18:9-14 SKITS

Desired Result:
To explore what Jesus teaches about prayer.
(Choose Option A, B, or C.)

Bible
(Allow 12 minutes.)

Have the youth form two teams. Assign Luke 18:1-8 to one team and Luke 18:9-14 to the other team. Ask each team to write a contemporary version of their passage and make it into a skit. Have the teams perform their skits. After each skit **ASK:**

➤ **What does this passage teach about the way Jesus wanted the disciples to pray?**

➤ **What does it say to you about the ways you can pray today?**

Read aloud Luke 18:1-14.

B LORD'S PRAYER WALLPAPER

roll of white freezer paper or wrapping paper, markers, King James Bible, New Revised Standard Bible, *any other translations of the Bible that are available, YouthPage*
(Allow 10 minutes.)

Ahead of time write the traditional version of the Lord's Prayer in one continuous line across a long edge of freezer paper. Tape this to a wall or a long table top so that it is easily accessible to the youth.

Have one youth read aloud Matthew 6:9-13 in the *King James Bible*, one read this passage in the *New Revised Standard Bible*, and one read it in the *New International Bible, Today's English Bible*, or other translations that are available in addition to *King James* and *New Revised Standard*. Do the same thing with Luke 11:2-4. Tell or read the information about the Lord's Prayer on the Read Me page.

Have the youth illustrate each part of the Lord's Prayer beneath where it is written on the freezer paper. The result will be a long section of "wallpaper."

C PRAY FOR ALL CHRISTIANS

prayer cube created in activity 3C, small table, Bible, small cross, a candle in a candle holder and matches
(Allow 5 minutes.)

If you created the prayer cube in activity 3C, place it on or near an altar, made by placing a Bible, a small cross, and a candle in a candle holder on a small table.

SAY:
➤ **Jesus prayed for the disciples. Come to the altar. Look again at the prayer cube to identify what Jesus prayed for. Let Jesus' prayer open your heart to pray for all Christians in our world.**

Let the youth spend about three to five minutes in silent prayer. Close the day's session with the "Closing Connection" below.

CLOSING CONNECTION

Desired Result:
To worship together.

hymnal (or other source for "Thy Word is a Lamp" [or similar hymn])
(Allow 5 minutes.)

SING A PRAYER

Have the youth gather in a circle. Sing "Thy Word is a Lamp," or a similar song from your hymnal. If you are not musical, have the youth read the words as a prayer.

Close with the following prayer:

Thank you, Jesus, for teaching us how to pray. Help us to listen to your guiding words. Help us to pray as you want us to pray. Amen.

Read Me THIS IS WHAT YOU NEED TO KNOW ABOUT THE TOPIC.

PREPARING YOURSELF

Jesus' life and teachings provide a rich source of information for Christians about when, what, and how to pray. Take a moment before you consider the teachings of Jesus to think about what you already know about prayer. How do you think Jesus wants you to pray?

Read the Bible passages and the Bible Background below. How do these readings enhance or change your understanding of Jesus' teachings about prayer?

Do for yourself the "What's in your Closet" activity on the YouthPage.

➤ **What actual place or space might serve as a "closet" where you can pray in secret?**

➤ **In what ways are your thoughts and feelings like a closet? different from a closet?**

➤ **What insights did you gain about your feelings and about God's acceptance and love for you as you are?**

Think about the youth in your group. Consider ways you can encourage them to pray. How might you help them experience God's love and acceptance through prayer?

1.

2.

3.

4.

GET READY

Bible Background

Matthew 6:5-8 encourages those who pray to avoid using prayer to draw attention to themselves by making sure they can be seen, or by praying a long time with flowery words. Public or private prayer is a matter of relating to God with one's heart and mind, not to one's need to be noticed by other people.

Luke's Gospel tells us that Jesus prayed often, especially at decisive moments in his life. He prayed at his baptism where he was initiated into his ministering role as the Son of God (Luke 3:21). He often withdrew to pray to find the resources he needed to heal and to teach the people (Luke 5:15-16). Before he called the disciples, he went to a mountain and spent the night in prayer (Luke 6:12). Peter and John witnessed his transfiguration as he prayed on a mountain (Luke 9:29). He brought his fears to God and gained strength as he prayed in Gethsemane (Luke 22:39-46). As he hung on the cross he prayed for God to forgive those who crucified him and expressed his final trust in God at the moment of his death (Luke 23:34, 46). Jesus' entire ministry was undergirded with a rich prayer life which expressed a close, familial relationship with God.

In Luke 22:39-46, immediately before his arrest, Jesus prayed. The scene is vivid and full of poignant details. We learn that prayer was his custom and that his friends accompanied him (v. 39). He instructs his friends to pray for their safety (v. 40). He feels the burden of his own fear, yet seeks God's will as the means for moving through his fear (v. 42). He discovers God's gift of strength through prayer (v. 43). Prayer gives him an opportunity to offer his intense anguish to God (v. 44). When he awakens the disciples, he once again advises them to pray (v. 45). Prayer is the means through which Jesus gains the strength he needs even in the midst of his anguish.

In John 17 Jesus prays for the disciples. He asks that God reveal the Son's glory to them and give them eternal life, protection, joy, knowledge of the truth of God's word, unity, and the love of God.

The Lord's Prayer is found in Matthew 6:9-13 and Luke 11:2-4. The traditional memorized version comes from the King James version of the Bible and includes a doxology or statement of praise that is not in the oldest and best manuscripts of Matthew's Gospel. It is, however, a fitting and heartfelt way to end the prayer given by Jesus. The prayer names God as one who is close to us and who is holy and totally other than us at the same time. It encourages praying for God's will, for provision of essential needs one day at a time, for forgiveness based upon the ability to forgive others, and for protection from evil and temptation.

WHAT'S IN YOUR CLOSET?

Jesus told the disciples not to pray in order to be seen or in order to try to impress others. He said "go into your room and shut the door and pray to your Father, who is in secret;" (Matthew 6:6).

The Greek word for "room" (tameion) actually means a storage room or closet.

➤ **What do you keep in your closet?**

➤ **Would you want to go in there to pray? Why or why not?**

➤ **Why do you think Jesus told the disciples to pray in a closet?**

THE K.I.S.S. RULE—
KEEP IT SIMPLE AND SINCERE.

Jesus criticized those who prayed a long time with lots of flowery words (Matthew 6:7-8). He said "Don't be like them." He might tell us to follow the K.I.S.S. rule! Keep your prayers simple and sincere. Let the focus be on God rather than on trying to impress people.

WHAT DID JESUS DO?

Look up the following passages in the Bible. What was going on? What did Jesus do in each situation?

____

____

____

____

____

____

____

Luke 3:21	Luke 5:15-16	Luke 6:12
Luke 9:29	Luke 22:39-46	Luke 23:34, 46

THE LORD'S PRAYER

"Pray then in this way: Our Father in heaven, hallowed be your name. Your kingdom come. Your will be done, on earth as it is in heaven. Give us this day our daily bread. And forgive us our debts, as we also have forgiven our debtors. And do not bring us to the time of trial, but rescue us from the evil one" (Matthew 6:9-13).

SESSION 3

WHAT DIFFERENCE DOES PRAYER MAKE?

FOCUS

To explore ways the practice of prayer makes a difference in our lives and in the world.

SCRIPTURE

Psalms 4:3-6; 150; Isaiah 1:15-17; Hosea 6:6; Amos 5:21-24; Micah 6:8; Matthew 6:12; Mark 11:23-25; Luke 11:9-13; 18:1-9

HERE'S THE PLAN | **DO IT YOUR WAY**

OPTIONS	TIME (minutes)	PREPARATION	SUPPLIES
INITIAL CONNECTION			
A Positive Prayers	10		paper, markers, masking tape
B Pray Psalm 150	5		Bible
CONNECT WITH THE SESSION			
A Identify Ways to Pray	8	make copies of YouthPage	YouthPage, Read Me
B Body Prayer	8	make copies of YouthPage	YouthPage, Read Me, Bibles
CONNECT WITH THE BIBLE AND THE FAITH COMMUNITY			
A Luke 18:1-8 Giant Comic Strip	12		Bible, large sheet of newsprint or a roll of freezer paper, markers
B Knocking on God's Door	8	make copies of YouthPage	YouthPage, Bible
C Fish or Snake	10	cut out large & small fish	YouthPage, roll of freezer paper, one die from a pair of dice, poster paper.
CONNECT WITH LIFE			
A Scripture & Phrases	8	copy phrases onto paper strips & Scripture onto posterboard	tape, poster paper, markers
B Identify Mountains	5	make copies of YouthPage	YouthPage, Bible
CLOSING CONNECTION			
A Pray for "Fish"	5		fish cutouts, table, candle, Bible, matches
B Pray for Others	5		small pieces of paper, basket

INITIAL CONNECTION

A POSITIVE PRAYERS

Desired Result:
To enjoy social interaction and physical activity and to begin thinking about the positive effects of prayer. **(Choose Option A or B.)**

paper, markers, masking tape
(Allow 10 minutes.)

Tape a sheet of paper to each youth's back. Give each youth a marker. Tell the youth they are to write a positive, uplifting prayer sentence on each person's back. Help them get started by suggesting that they fill in the blanks of the following sentence "(name), I pray that you ____________." After everyone has written a prayer sentence on every back, sit in a circle and have each youth tell what others have written.

ASK:

- **What was it like to think of an uplifting prayer for another person?**
- **What feelings do you have when you read the positive prayers written for you?**
- **Do you think the prayer sentences had an effect on your feelings? Why or why not?**

B PRAY PSALM 150

Bible
(Allow 5 minutes.)

Read aloud Psalm 150. Assign the following to five teams of youth: trumpets, lutes and harps, tambourines and dance, strings and pipes, cymbals. Tell the youth to mime their part when they hear it. Read Psalm 150 again with lots of enthusiasm. If you have a small group, have all the youth mime each of the parts.

ASK:

- **Did this reading of Psalm 150 seem like prayer to you? Why or why not?**
- **How did this way of praying affect your feelings? Your thoughts about God?**

CONNECT WITH THE SESSION

Desired Result:
To explore ways to pray as tools to open one's heart and mind to God's love and guidance through Christ.
(Choose Option A or B.)

YouthPage, Read Me
(Allow 8 minutes.)

IDENTIFY WAYS TO PRAY

Have a youth read aloud the material entitled "Many Ways to Pray" on the YouthPage. Tell in your own words the information in "Many Ways to Pray" from the Read Me page. Have the youth write other ways to pray in the space provided on the YouthPage.

Tell the youth you are going to lead them through several different ways of praying. Have them close their eyes and be silent. Pray as follows:

"Loving God, help us find new ways to be closer to you through Christ as we explore these ways to pray." Continue as follows: **"Be very silent and still. Simply listen.** (Allow a few seconds.) **Pay attention to your breath. Feel the air go into your lungs. Pay attention to how it feels when you breathe out again. As you breathe in, say silently the word "love."**

As you breathe out, say silently the word "peace." Pay attention to the way you feel. As you breathe in, move your hands slowly to your chest and place them over your heart. As you breathe out, open your arms slowly as though you are welcoming someone. Pay attention to the way you feel.

(Allow a few seconds.) **Imagine that you are in a special, safe place with Jesus. Notice where you are. Fill in the details of the scene. You want to ask Jesus something. What do you ask? What does Jesus say?** (Allow a few seconds.) **Say goodbye to Jesus, knowing that you can return anytime you wish. Become aware of this room. When you feel ready, open your eyes.**

When all the youth have opened their eyes, **ASK:**

- **What was it like to simply listen to God?**
- **What was it like to pay attention to your breathing?**
- **What was it like to say the words "love" and "peace" as you breathed in and out?**
- **What was it like to gesture with your arms and hands?**
- **What was it like to imagine that you were in a special place with Jesus?**
- **What did you learn about prayer as you used all these different methods?**

BODY PRAYER

YouthPage, Read Me, Bibles
(Allow 8 minutes.)

Have a youth read aloud the material entitled "Many Ways to Pray" on the YouthPage. Tell in your own words the information in "Many Ways to Pray" from the Read Me pages. Have the youth write others ways to pray in the space provided on the YouthPage.

Demonstrate a Great Commandment body prayer (Matthew 22:37-40) as follows:

• Stand.

• Say "Love" and raise your hands and arms up toward heaven.

• Say "the Lord Your God," and at the same time, lower your hands to your sides forming wide arcs out from your sides as you lower them.

• Say "with all your heart, soul, and mind," and at the same time, raise your hands slowly and rest them on your heart.

• Say "Love your neighbor" and at the same time reach straight out in front of you as though welcoming someone.

• Say "as you love yourself" and at the same time, return your hands to your heart.

Invite the youth to do this prayer with you.

Have the youth form two teams. Tell each team to choose a Bible passage and make up a body prayer to go with it. If they have difficulty finding a Bible passage, suggest Psalms 147 and 148.

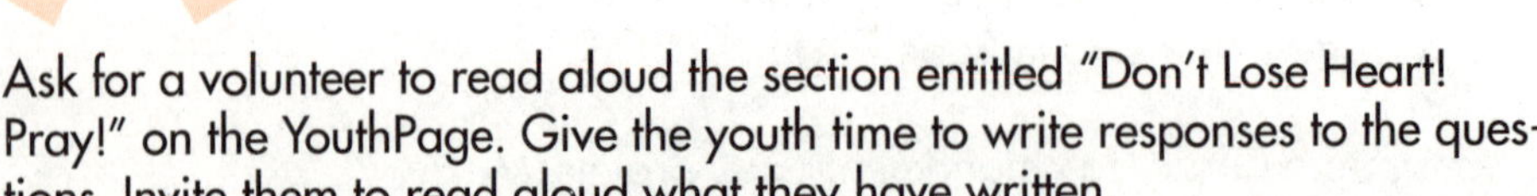

CONNECT WITH THE BIBLE AND THE FAITH COMMUNITY

Desired Result:
To explore what the Bible says about the results of prayer.
(Choose Option A, B, or C.)

YouthPage, Bible, large sheet of newsprint or a roll of freezer paper, markers
(Allow 12 minutes.)

A CREATE A GIANT COMIC STRIP OF LUKE 18:1-8

Ask for a volunteer to read aloud the section entitled "Don't Lose Heart! Pray!" on the YouthPage. Give the youth time to write responses to the questions. Invite them to read aloud what they have written.

Read aloud Luke 18:1-8. Have the youth create a comic strip of the story of the widow and the unjust judge by sketching in three or four scenes and using "balloons" for the dialogue.

ASK:

- **How is God different from the unjust judge?**
- **How can you be more like the widow as you pray?**
- **What did the widow want?**
- **Judging from the story, what do you think God desires regarding justice?**

YouthPage, Bible
(Allow 8 minutes.)

B DISCUSS KNOCKING ON GOD'S DOOR

Read aloud Luke 11:9-10. Read aloud the activity in the section entitled "Knock, and the Door Will Be Opened for You" on the YouthPage. Invite the youth to respond to the questions in this section.

roll of freezer paper, one die from a pair of dice, poster paper
(Allow 10 minutes.)

C FISH OR SNAKE

Ahead of time cut the posterboard into the shape of a large fish. Cut a small fish for each youth from the scraps of the posterboard or from other paper. Unroll the freezer paper and draw lines across it to divide it into squares large enough for a youth to stand on. Draw at least ten squares.

Have the youth identify something they would like to have, and write or draw it on the "fish."

Read aloud Luke 11:11-13. Tell them they are going to play a giant board game. The object is to get to their "fish." They will throw the die and walk the number of squares indicated on the die. If they throw a two, they have gotten a "snake" and must sit down. If they throw a six, they go all the way to their "fish."

After the game, give each youth a small cutout of a fish. **ASK:**

➤ **What is a "fish" or special need that you would like to pray for?**

Have them write these on the small fish. Tell them to save these for use in the closing worship.

CONNECT WITH LIFE

SCRIPTURES AND PHRASES

Desired Result:
To explore the scriptural requirements for justice, righteousness, forgiveness, and faith as one prays.
(Choose Option A or B.)

poster paper, markers, tape
(Allow 8 minutes.)

Ahead of time, cut some strips of posterboard. Write the following phrases on the strips, one phrase to a strip:

do good	seek justice	rescue the oppressed
defend the orphan	plead for the widow	forgive
believe	let justice and righteousness roll	
do justice	walk humbly with your God	love kindness
have clean hands and pure hearts		

Write the following Scriptures on a poster or on large white paper.

Isaiah 1:15-17	Psalm 24:1-6	Amos 5:21-24
Mark 11:23-25	Micah 6:8	Matthew 6:12

Have the youth read the Bible passages and then match a phrase to the passage. They will tape the phrase beside the Scripture it best matches. When all the phrases are matched to Scriptures, **ASK:**

➤ **What do all these texts say to you about God's expectations of those who pray?**

➤ **What do they say to you about ways God might answer prayer?**

IDENTIFY MOUNTAINS

YouthPage, Bible
(Allow 5 minutes.)

Have a youth read aloud Mark 11:23-24, and the section entitled "Moving Mountains" from the Youth Page. Allow time for the youth to write responses to the questions. Invite the youth to pray silently about the mountains in their llives.

CLOSING CONNECTION

Desired Result:
To focus the youth on prayer for others.
(Choose Option A or B.)

PRAY FOR "FISH"

fish created in option 3C, small table, cross, candle in a candle holder, matches, Bible
(Allow 5 minutes.)

Create a "sacred space" by making a small altar. Place the candle, cross, and Bible on the table. Be creative. You or the youth may have special things you would like to put on the altar. Have the youth gather with you near the altar. Invite the youth to bring their "fish" or special need to the altar. Pray as follows:

Loving God, thank you for hearing our prayers. We bring our "fish" to you knowing you will answer our prayers in the best way for us.

(Invite youth to pray for the need written on their fish. Any who wish to pray aloud may do so. Close the time of prayer as follows.)

In the name of Jesus, who told us to believe, we pray. Amen.

PRAY FOR OTHERS

small pieces of paper, basket
(Allow 5 minutes.)

Have the youth stand in a circle. Invite the youth to name a person or issue they want to pray for. Write these on small pieces of paper and place them in a basket. Have each youth draw one of the pieces of paper out of the basket. Tell them to pray silently or aloud for that need. Begin the time of prayer as follows:

O God, we know that you care for all these people and issues. So do we.

Allow time for youth to pray aloud. Close the time of prayer as follows:

Thank you for accepting our prayers and our concern; in the love and care of Christ we pray. Amen.

Read Me

THIS IS WHAT YOU NEED TO KNOW ABOUT THE TOPIC.

PREPARING YOURSELF

Create a "sacred space" for prayer and reflection on this session. You may have a favorite chair or a special corner of your room. Light a candle if it helps you open yourself to God. Write down your thoughts and answers to the questions below in the spaces provided.

Read "Many Ways to Pray." What new insights did you gain about prayer?

Read the Bible Passages. What expectations do you think God has of you as you pray?

Think about your class. Who are the youth? How do you think you might help them want to pray more? Write some ideas below:

MANY WAYS TO PRAY

The Christian tradition teaches many ways to pray. All ways of prayer have the goal of helping one experience close communion with God. The ways to pray may be thought of as "tools" or techniques that assist true prayer rather than prayer itself. True Christian prayer is the opening of the heart and mind to God's presence and will through Jesus Christ.

Opening to God can be done by talking to God, either silently or aloud. One can meditate or focus the mind on an object, thought, Bible verse, or anything else in order to pay closer attention to God's presence.

Repetition of a prayer sentence like the Jesus Prayer (Lord Jesus Christ, have mercy on me, a sinner.), or a favorite Bible verse helps a person open to God. Some Christians use contemplation or silence, the intentional emptying of the mind of all thoughts and images in order to simply listen to or be with God who is beyond all thought. Others use God's gift of imagination to help them pray.

Charismatic Christians often pray in teams and lay hands on or near one another in order to experience gifts like praying in tongues, resting in God's Spirit, healing, and knowing God's will.

Body gestures like kneeling, sitting, standing, raising the arms, or placing the hands in a variety of positions assist prayer. One may also assist prayer by doing some stretching exercises or by synchronizing the stretching with memorized Scripture or the Lords's Prayer. Using stretches helps to relax a person so that they can be more available to God.

Sacred spaces help bring awareness to God. Some people create their own sacred space using special objects like candles or music to help them enter a prayerful mood. Religious music, literature, and art often inspire a prayerful awareness. A church sanctuary is helpful to many. Still others go to a favorite spot in the outdoor world.

Some Christians offer to God every task they perform during a day. For such people, life is a gift to be returned to God.

All such prayer tools should be used with the intent of opening to God through Jesus Christ. When used for this purpose, they are valuable aids to Christian prayer. No one tool is the only right or wrong way. People must choose a way to pray that is the most helpful for them as they seek to be with God.

WHAT DOES THE LORD REQUIRE?

BIBLE BACKGROUND

Christians who want to grow spiritually must encounter the issue of apparently "unanswered" prayer. Sometimes things do not turn out the way we expect or desire. We are tempted to "lose heart" or to believe that prayer does no good. The Bible helps sort through such issues.

In Luke 18:1-8, Jesus encouraged those with such feelings to be persistent in prayer. He told a story about a widow who sought justice from an unjust judge. The character of the judge is set in direct contrast to God, who is good. The judge grants the woman's request because she pestered him. In direct contrast to the judge, God is good. God desires justice for the people. Therefore, says Jesus, pray! God is faithful.

A similar story in Luke 11:5-10 sets human nature again in contrast to the nature of God. Even a friend who does not wish to be disturbed will respond to persistence. God, who is good, provides for those who seek, who ask, who pray. God willingly opens the door to those who knock.

God may not give what we ask for but God always gives what we need. God also has some expectations from us. The prophets taught that prayer is more than ritual. Those who pray are expected to attend to matters of justice and righteousness (Psalms 24:1-6; Isaiah 1:15-17; Amos 5:21-24; Micah 6:8). The Lord's Prayer calls for forgiveness only on the basis of forgiving others (Matthew 6:12; Mark 11:25). Jesus called for faith to undergird prayer (Mark 11:23-25).

These ethical and spiritual matters have the effect of transforming the one who prays. Perhaps the real answer to prayer rests within this transformation. What the Lord requires leads to wholeness and peace for oneself and one's neighbor.

MANY WAYS TO PRAY

The Christian tradition teaches that there are many ways to pray. Ways to pray are tools that help the mind and heart stay focused on Christ.

- Talking to God
- Silently listening to God
- Praying a psalm
- Praying memorized prayers
- Reading a responsive litany
- Imagining a scene from Scripture
- Repeating a prayer sentence or Bible verse
- Praying in a special place
- Listening to religious music
- Using special body gestures or positions
- Can you think of other ways to pray? Write them here.

DON'T LOSE HEART! PRAY!

Have you ever prayed for something but didn't get it? How did you feel? What did you think?

Think of a time when you "lost heart" and decided not to pray because you didn't think it would do any good. Write about it below.

Imagine that you are standing in front of this door.
You want to knock because you believe God is on the other side.

➤ **Why do you want to knock on the door?**

➤ **What do you think will happen if you knock on the door?**

➤ **What does Jesus say about knocking on the door?**

➤ **What do you think Jesus means when he says "the door will be opened for you?"**

MOVING MOUNTAINS

Have you ever experienced something in your life that seemed like an immovable mountain blocking your way? What was it? Identify a mountain that exists in your life now. Write about it inside the mountain.

Jesus assures us that if we believe, our mountains will be moved (Mark 11:23). Trust clears away the fear that blocks our ability to act. What is one thing you can begin to do this week to move your mountain?

SHAPING OUR FAITH

© MIMI FORSYTH

SESSION 1: FAITH: THE JOURNEY BEGINS
SESSION 2: FAITH: A LIFE-LONG JOURNEY

Purpose

This unit will help young teens define faith and identify how faith impacts everyday life.

This Is Not Junk Mail!

IT'S IMPORTANT STUFF FROM YOUR TEENAGER'S SUNDAY MORNING LEADER

It's true! This means that the time to introduce and discuss issues of faith with your teen is now.

Until now, your young person has relied on the significant others in life (parents, teachers, counselors) to tell and retell the stories of faith that permeate the Bible. It is during adolescence that young people begin to develop a set of personal beliefs and begin to shape their faith journey. They may begin to question ideas that they merely accepted as fact during their childhood. Faith is born out of doubt, and it is important for parents to offer youth the opportunity to explore these abstract concepts in an effort to develop a concrete belief system. Through this process, young people have an opportunity to become part of the story and integrate their faith into their everyday lives.

This unit will help young people define faith and identify how faith impacts everyday life.

TABLE TALK

Does Faith Matter? Talk with your youth about how your faith impacts your own life.

Did you know that of all adults who profess to have faith today, most made that commitment as a teenager?

Often we assume that this is evident to our families, but many times we need to hear faith defined in words. Keep it simple and honest.

FAITH IS A JOURNEY

Your youth will be creating a "Faith Map" which looks at the significant events of their life and whether they realized God's presence during that time.

HOW CAN I STRENGTHEN MY FAITH?

Share with your youth ways that your faith is strengthened. If shaping your faith is a life long process for you, then your young person will have the best guide possible leading the way.

Share some high and low moments in your life. Did you feel that God was with you?

Hallelujah!

IDEAS FOR PEOPLE WHO PLAN WORSHIP

The following ideas may be used for times of worship or celebration during your class session. You may also share these suggestions with your pastor, choir director, and worship work-area chairperson to help them discover ideas and resources for making worship more youth-friendly.

MUSIC SUGGESTIONS

How Firm a Foundation
Hymn of Promise
Lonely the Boat
Have Thine Own Way, Lord
Faith of Our Fathers

PRAYERS FOR FAITH

Lord Jesus**, open our eyes that we might see you in our lives today. Help us to have faith in you. **Amen.

***Lord**, we do not ask for a mountain of faith—only for a mustard seed. Fill us with an assurance of your love. May our faith in you transform us so that we might transform the world. **Amen**.*

SCRIPTURE SUGGESTIONS

- Mark 4:31-35
- Romans 12:1-2
- Hebrews 11:1-3

Stress the creed's emphasis upon God's presence in our world—whether or not we actually see God.

The World Methodist Social Affirmation

We believe in God, creator of the world and of all people;
and in Jesus Christ, incarnate among us,
who died and rose again;
and in the Holy Spirit,
present with us to guide, strengthen, and comfort.

We believe;
God, help our unbelief.

We rejoice in every sign of God's kingdom:
in the upholding of human dignity and community;
in every expression of love, justice, and reconciliation;
in each act of self-giving on behalf of others;
in the abundance of God's gifts
entrusted to us that all may have enough;
in all responsible use of the earth's resources

Glory be to God on high;
and on earth, peace.

We confess our sin, individual and collective,
by silence of action:
through the violation of human dignity
based on race, class, age, sex, nation, or faith;
through the exploitation of people
because of greed and indifference;
through the misuse of power
in personal, communal, national, and international life;
through the search for security
by those military and economic forces
that threaten human existence;
through the abuse of technology
which endangers the earth and all life upon it.

Lord, have mercy;
Christ, have mercy;
Lord, have mercy.

We commit ourselves individually and as a community
to the way of Christ:
to take up the cross;
to seek abundant life for all humanity;
to struggle for peace with justice and freedom;
to risk ourselves in faith, hope, and love,
praying that God's kingdom may come.

Thy kingdom come on earth as it is in heaven. Amen.

SERMON ILLUSTRATIONS

Faith involves risk. Are we willing to put our actions where our words have been?

There is a story of a great tightrope walker who planned to cross Niagara Falls. On the appointed day, a crowd gathered to watch his attempt. The crowd cheered noisily as the tightrope walker neared the rope. He asked the crowd if they supported him and believed that he could successfully cross the wire, and the crowd roared their support. He asked if they believed that he could cross the wire pushing a wheelbarrow. Again, they roared in support. He asked if they believed that he could cross the line pushing a wheelbarrow with a person in the wheelbarrow, at which time the crowd went wild. "Yes!" They believed in him. The tightrope walker's next question was simple and direct: "Since you believe completely in my ability to cross the wire, who will volunteer to climb into the wheelbarrow to be pushed across?" The crowd grew silent and then dispersed.

SERMON ILLUSTRATIONS

There is a story concerning an eagle's egg that fell into a chicken's nest. The mother hen hatched all the eggs in the nest and raised the eaglet as if he were her own. The eaglet never knew that he was an eagle and not a chicken until another bird shared the news. The eaglet did not believe the other bird; how could he be able to soar above the clouds like an eagle? After all, he had never been raised to do that. He spent his life wishing that he could fly like an eagle and believing that he was limited to the life of a chicken.

Faith in Christ empowers us to be transformed into what God knows that we can be. Like the eagle who believed himself to be a chicken, we may believe that we can never be Christ-like. But the truth is that faith sets us free to be who we are meant to be. Faith helps us become more Christ-like.

Miscellany

IDEAS FOR TEACHERS

The stages of faith development can vary greatly from person to person and from age to age. In addition to the physical and emotional diversity between junior and senior highs, their spiritual formation may be worlds apart. However, this could also provide some very teachable moments during this unit as the focus will be on the fact that faith is a life-long journey rather than a one-time experience

It will be very important in a multi-age class to work in small groups so that all members of the class will feel comfortable enough to share their questions and ideas.

The focus will be on the fact that faith is a life-long journey rather than a one-time experience.

As you divide the class into small groups for various activities, be sure senior high youth are in each group in order to provide leadership and also to demonstrate to the younger youth that faith is a growth process that will impact every area of their life. The younger youth look to the senior highs as role models and will learn a lot from hearing their story.

In turn, the senior highs will be able to reflect on the growth in their own lives as they hear the stories shared by the younger youth.

It will be very important in a multi-age class to work in small groups so that all members of the class will feel comfortable enough to share their questions and ideas. In a large group, the younger youth may be intimidated by the older youth unless a sense of community is established.

Keep the Faith

SESSION 1:

FAITH: THE JOURNEY BEGINS

FOCUS

Everyone believes in something, and what we put our faith in defines who we are.

SCRIPTURE

Hebrews 11:1-3

HERE'S THE PLAN | DO IT YOUR WAY

OPTIONS	TIME (minutes)	PREPARATION	SUPPLIES
INITIAL CONNECTION			
A Graffiti Sheet	8-10	prepare poster	newsprint or poster board, masking tape, markers or pens, Bible
B Define Faith	8-10		index cards, pencils, chalkboard and chalk or newsprint and marker, Bible
C Faith Comparisons	12-15	make copies of Youth Page	YouthPage, pencils, chalkboard and chalk or newsprint and marker, Bible
CONNECT WITH THE SESSION			
A Group Challenge	7-10		paper and markers, Bible
B What Don't You See?	8-10		chalkboard and chalk or newsprint and marker, Bible
C Believe It or Not	12-15	make list of unseen items	Bible
CONNECT WITH THE BIBLE AND THE FAITH COMMUNITY			
A Who Do You Trust?	7-9	make copies of Youth Page	YouthPage, pencils, Bible
B Stand Up	7-9	make copies of Youth Page	YouthPage, Bible
CONNECT WITH LIFE			
A Lean on Me	12-15		
B Walk of Faith	8-10		blindfolds
C I Trust Because...	6-8		paper and pencil, chalkboard and chalk or newsprint and marker
CLOSING CONNECTION			
A Pray Together	2-3	prepare prayer ahead of time	
B Open-Eye Prayer	1-2	make copies of Youth Page	YouthPage

Desired Result:
To come to a group understanding of the definition of faith.
(Choose Option A, B, or C.)

INITIAL CONNECTION

A GRAFFITI SHEET

newsprint or poster board, masking tape, markers or pens, Bible
(Allow 8-10 minutes.)

Before class, write the words "Faith Is..." on a large sheet of newsprint or poster board and tape paper to wall. As students enter, have each add responses, words, comments or pictures to the page. Discuss the responses, coming to consensus on a definition of faith from what was written and what is said. Record the definition for all to see.

State that the Bible seldom defines words and concepts; however, the Bible does offer a specific definition of faith. Read Hebrews 11:1-3, restating the meaning of these verses in your own words. Allow time for questions and comments.

B DEFINE FAITH

index cards, pencils, chalkboard and chalk or newsprint and marker, Bible
(Allow 8-10 minutes.)

As youth enter, give each an index card and a pencil. Have youth write a definition of faith. Take up cards and read. Allow time for comments after each response. Come to consensus on a definition of faith. Record the definition for all to see.

State that the Bible seldom defines words and concepts; however, the Bible does offer a specific definition of faith. Read Hebrews 11:1-3, restating the meaning of these verses in your own words. Allow time for questions and comments.

C FAITH COMPARISONS

YouthPage, pencils, chalkboard and chalk or newsprint and marker, Bible
(Allow 12-15 minutes.)

Have youth complete *Faith Comparisons* from the Youthpage. Discuss each comparison, asking youth to share why they responded as they did.

As a group, come up with a definition of faith. Record the definition on newsprint or chalkboard for all to see.

State that the Bible seldom defines words and concepts; however, the Bible does offer a specific definition of faith. Read Hebrews 11:1-3, restating the meaning of the verses in your own words. Allow time for questions and comments.

CONNECT WITH THE SESSION

GROUP CHALLENGE

A

Form groups of three or four youth. Give each group paper and marker. Have teams name as many things as they can think of in which they believe but cannot see (such as the wind). After three or four minutes, call time, and have each group share its list. After each response **ASK:**

➤ **Why do you believe in that?** or **What does it take to believe in that?** Award one point for each item not listed by another group. Congratulate each group for teamwork and point out the "winning team" as the team having the most points.

SAY:

➤ **There are many things in which we believe but cannot see.** Remind the group of Hebrews 11:1. State that one definition of faith is believing in what we cannot see.

Desired Result:
To affirm that we all believe in something, even some things that are unseen. **(Choose Option A, B, or C.)**

paper and markers, Bible
(Allow 7-10 minutes.)

WHAT DON'T YOU SEE?

B

As a group, brainstorm and list ideas of items in which you believe but you cannot see. After each response, **ASK:**

➤ **Why do you believe in that?** or

➤ **What does it take to believe in that?**

SAY: There are many things which we cannot see or touch in which we believe. Remind the group of Hebrews 11:1. State that one definition of faith is believing in what we cannot see.

chalkboard and chalk or newsprint and marker, Bible
(Allow 8-10 minutes.)

BELIEVE IT OR NOT

C

Before class, come up with a list of things you believe to exist but that you cannot see. (Examples: wind, air, gravity, love, energy, God, outer space) Ask for volunteers to act out each item and have the group guess what they are acting out. After each correct guess, **ASK** the group,

Bible
(Allow 12-15 minutes.)

➤ **Why do you believe in that?** or **What does it take to believe in that?**

SAY:

➤ **There are many things we believe in that we cannot see or touch.** Remind the group of Hebrews 11:1. State that one definition of faith is believing in what we cannot see.

CONNECT WITH THE BIBLE AND THE FAITH COMMUNITY

Desired Result: To consider who we trust and why. **(Choose Option A or B.)**

A WHO DO YOU TRUST?

YouthPage, pencils, Bible ***(Allow 7-9 minutes.)***

Instruct youth to complete "Who Do You Trust?" from the YouthPage.

As a large group, discuss the activity, asking for responses and reasons for each response. **ASK:**

➤ **Who is the easiest person to trust? Why?**

➤ **Who is the most difficult to trust? Why?**

Point out that past experience affects our trust level. State that even persons deserving of trust don't always receive it. Read Mark 4:35-41. **ASK:**

➤ **Why might the disciples not have had faith in Jesus?**

➤ **How do you think the disciples felt when Jesus rebuked them?**

➤ **What would have helped the disciples to have more faith in Jesus?**

➤ **How is this story like or unlike your situation?**

B STAND UP

YouthPage, Bible ***(Allow 7-9 minutes.)***

Read aloud the list of persons from "Who Do You Trust?" on the YouthPage activity. Designate spots in the room which stand for each response. (For example: to the far left is **always**, to the left center is **almost always**, etc.) Have youth respond to each statement by moving to the area of the room which matches their response. Discuss responses.

Point out that past experience affects our trust level.

State that even persons deserving of trust don't always receive it. Read Mark 4:35-41. **ASK:**

➤ **Why might the disciples not have had faith in Jesus?**

➤ **How do you think the disciples felt when Jesus rebuked them?**

➤ **What would have helped the disciples to have more faith in Jesus? How is this story like or unlike your situation?**

CONNECT WITH LIFE

Desired Result:
To test our ability to trust others.
(Choose Option A or B.)

LEAN ON ME

A

(Allow 12-15 minutes.)

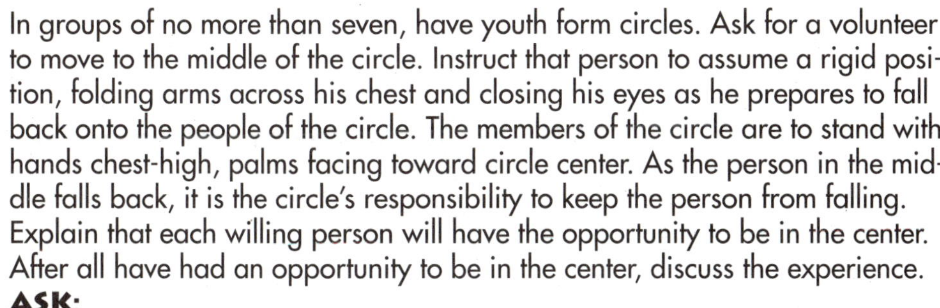

In groups of no more than seven, have youth form circles. Ask for a volunteer to move to the middle of the circle. Instruct that person to assume a rigid position, folding arms across his chest and closing his eyes as he prepares to fall back onto the people of the circle. The members of the circle are to stand with hands chest-high, palms facing toward circle center. As the person in the middle falls back, it is the circle's responsibility to keep the person from falling. Explain that each willing person will have the opportunity to be in the center. After all have had an opportunity to be in the center, discuss the experience. **ASK:**

➤ **How did you feel to be the person who had to trust others?**

➤ **How did it feel to be the person who was trusted?**

➤ **What were the responsibilities of each person? What were the risks?**

State that strengthening one's faith requires trust as well as risk.

WALK OF FAITH

B

blindfolds
(Allow 8-10 minutes.)

Pair off, giving a blindfold to the person who lives closest to the church. Instruct that person to put on the blindfold so that he or she cannot see. The other person becomes the guide who leads the blindfolded individual on a walk of faith—guiding them around, through, or under whatever obstacles they choose. Switch positions and repeat the activity.

Discuss the experience by asking questions such as:

➤ **How did it feel to be the blindfolded partner?**

➤ **How did it feel to be the guide?**

➤ **What were the responsibilities? What were the risks?**

State that strengthening one's faith requires trust as well as risk.

paper and pencil, chalkboard and chalk or newsprint and marker
(Allow 6-8 minutes.)

C I TRUST YOU BECAUSE...

Have each youth think about his or her best friend and list the qualities of that friend that makes for trustworthiness. Share responses with the total group. List the different responses for all to see. **ASK:**

➤ **What are the risks of trusting another person? What are the benefits?**

State that strengthening one's faith requires trust as well as risk.

CLOSING CONNECTION

Desired Result:
To affirm that each of us can grow in faith.
(Choose Option A or B.)

(Allow 6-8 minutes.)

A PRAY TOGETHER

Gather the group into a circle. Close in leader-led prayer for stronger lives of faith.

YouthPage
(Allow 1-2 minutes.)

B OPEN-EYE PRAYER

Read together "A Prayer for Faith" from the YouthPage.

Read Me

THIS IS WHAT YOU NEED TO KNOW ABOUT THE TOPIC.

KEY IDEAS IN THIS SESSION

Thanks to a variety of life experiences, youth have learned not to trust what they cannot see and touch. Faced with issues like violence, drug abuse, and a future without a sound ecology, youth live in the present, while only dreaming for the future. They seem to have taken on the attitude of **"Prove it!"** Youth need to be reminded that not all reality can be proved by sight or touch. In fact, there are many realities that cannot be seen. Consider the wind—we cannot see it or touch it; we merely feel its presence.

Youth have learned not to trust what they cannot see and touch.

Youth long to know God and to be assured of faith. However, assurance of faith is not essential for the existence of faith.

Youth need to know that they are not alone in the struggles of the faith journey.

SCRIPTURAL BACKGROUND

The Gospel of Mark was written for a Gentile audience and is geared toward people with questions concerning faith. Their questions are similar to the questions of faith asked by our youth. It is a fast-paced book, including less dialogue and commentary than the other Gospels. The book moves quickly from one action scene to the next.

The story of the calming of the storm reveals the disciples' lack of understanding concerning Jesus. Although they trust him, their trust becomes shaky when a difficult situation intensifies.

TEACHER SUGGESTIONS

Read the story of the calming of the storm (Mark 4:35-41) as you prepare to teach. Pray for God's guidance in discovering God's message for you and the group. Think about times in your life when your faith has been shaky.

Pray for the youth of your group as they struggle throughout the week with issues of faith.

Prayer:

Oh Lord, increase my faith so that I might be a better servant for you. Help me to listen to the words of the youth as they share. Help me to see through their eyes and to hear through their ears so that we all might see and hear you anew this day. Amen.

Choose one word from each pair as a response to the question below.

Is your faith more like a ________ or a ________?

whisper	sonic boom
bonfire	flashlight
period	question mark
leaky faucet	waterfall
friend	teacher
mountain top	valley
song	story
pencil	magic marker

Who Do You Trust?

Indicate how often you put your trust in each person by checking the correct boxes with your responses.

RESPONSES:	NEVER	SELDOM	SOMETIMES	ALMOST ALWAYS	ALWAYS
Mother					
Father					
Teacher					
Brother/Sister					
Minister					
Youth Leader					
Coach					
Friend					
President					
Police Officer					
Jesus					

A Payer for Faith

Lord Jesus,
Open our eyes that we might see you in our lives today. Help us to have faith in you. Amen.

SESSION 2:

FAITH: A LIFE-LONG JOURNEY

FOCUS

As we strive to grow in faith, it is important to remember that faith is not a destination; faith is a journey.

SCRIPTURE

Romans 12:1-2

HERE'S THE PLAN | DO IT YOUR WAY

OPTIONS	TIME (minutes)	PREPARATION	SUPPLIES
INITIAL CONNECTION			
A Faith Sculpture	8-10		paper clips or pipe cleaners
B Bag Faith	10-12		magazines, glue, paper bags
CONNECT WITH THE SESSION			
A Life Map	10-12	make copies of YouthPage	YouthPage, pencils
B Faith Honor Roll	7-9		chalkboard and chalk or newsprint and markers
C Life Impact	8-10		chalkboard and chalk or newsprint and markers
CONNECT WITH THE BIBLE AND THE FAITH COMMUNITY			
A What Does the Bible Say?	5-7		Bibles, chalkboard and chalk or newsprint and markers
B Conformity Versus Transformation	5-7	prepare definitions for conformity & transformation	Bibles, chalkboard and chalk or newsprint and markers
C Re-Creation	10-12		Bibles, paper clips or pipe cleaners
CONNECT WITH LIFE			
A Card Commitment	3-5		index cards, pencils
B Objects of Faith	8-10		
CLOSING CONNECTION			
Group Prayer	2-3		

Desired Result:
To come up with a visual expression of personal faith.
(Choose Option A or B.)

INITIAL CONNECTION

FAITH SCULPTURE

A

paper clips or pipe cleaners
(Allow 8-10 minutes.)

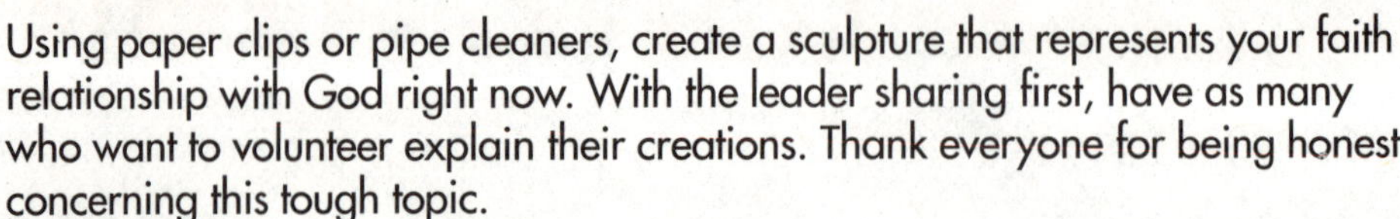

Using paper clips or pipe cleaners, create a sculpture that represents your faith relationship with God right now. With the leader sharing first, have as many who want to volunteer explain their creations. Thank everyone for being honest concerning this tough topic.

BAG FAITH

B

magazines, glue, paper bags
(Allow 10-12 minutes.)

As the youth enter, give each one a bag. Have a variety of magazines available. Instruct youth to browse through the magazines, finding words and pictures which represent faith and/or things in which they believe. Glue these to the outside of their bag. On the inside of the bag, instruct youth to place pictures and words representing questions they would like to ask God.

As the leader, you should tell the group about your bag and then invite the students to explain theirs.

CONNECT WITH THE SESSION

Desired Result:
To identify the impact of faith upon our lives.

LIFE MAPS

YouthPage, pencils
(Allow 10-12 minutes.)

Have youth complete the Life Map from the YouthPage.

In small groups of three or four, have youth share, beginning with the person who has the shortest middle name.

As a large group **ASK:**

➤ **When were you most aware of the presence of God?**

➤ **From your experience, does God seem more real in good times or in difficult times? Why?**

➤ **Can you name some of the times when you saw God in other people?**

Tell the students that although we do not see or feel God's presence at each and every moment of our lives, God is still there. Perhaps we do not see God because we are not looking for God or being open to God's presence.

FAITH HONOR ROLL

Have youth tell about one person who they believe possesses a strong faith. Ask what qualities are evident in his or her life? List the qualities and keep them on the classroom wall. When everyone who wants to has shared, compare the characteristics of a faith-filled life. List ideas for faithful living as a teen, and post it beside the other chart.

Chalkboard and chalk or newspaint and markers
(Allow 7-9 minutes.)

LIFE IMPACT

Ask youth to identify one person who has made a positive difference in their faith life, and to tell what difference they made. **ASK:**

➤ **What qualities are evident in this person's life?**

List qualities for all to see. When all have shared, compare the characteristics of a faith-filled life. List ideas for faithful living as a teen.

Chalkboard and chalk or newsprint and markers
(Allow 8-10 minutes.)

CONNECT WITH THE BIBLE AND THE FAITH COMMUNITY

WHAT DOES THE BIBLE SAY?

Desired Result:
To identify a Scripture that deals with growth in faith
(Choose Option A, B, or C.)

Ask the students to divide into groups, to individually read Romans 12:2, and then, as a group, restate this verse in everyday language.

List ideas for faithful living as a teen on chalkboard or newsprint.

Bibles, chalkboard and chalk or newsprint and markers
(Allow 5-7 minutes.)

CONFORMITY VERSUS TRANSFORMATION

Read Romans 12:2, and restate this verse in your own words. Discuss the differences between conformity and transformation. As a group, list qualities representing each. In groups of three to four, come up with a skit representing conformity or transformation.

List ideas for faithful living as a teen.

Bibles, chalkboard and chalk or newsprint and markers
(Allow 5-7 minutes.)

Bibles, paper clips or pipe cleaners
(Allow 10-12 minutes.)

RE-CREATION

Read Romans 12:2. Restate the verse in your own words, emphasizing that we have the power, with God's help, to be strengthened in faith. If your group created Faith Sculptures, have each person create a new sculpture representing one way in which they would like to see their faith grow.

CONNECT WITH LIFE

Desired Result:
To help youth experience faith as an ongoing part of life.

index cards, pencils
(Allow 3-5 minutes.)

CARD COMMITMENT

Pass out index cards. Have youth write down two or three areas in which they would like to see their faith grow. Place cards in center of circle. Close with prayer for God's strength, power and guidance.

(Allow 8-10 minutes.)

S

OBJECTS OF FAITH

Have youth locate, or decide upon, an object that symbolizes their faith. (If it is a pretty day, this would be a great opportunity to go outside.) Share with the group.

CLOSING CONNECTION

Desired Result:
To affirm that with God's help, we can grow in faith.

(Allow 2-3 minutes.)

PRAYER

Close with prayer asking for God's help for growing in faith.

Read Me

THIS IS WHAT YOU NEED TO KNOW ABOUT THE TOPIC.

Key Ideas in This Session

In this fast paced and ever-changing world, young people are searching and hungering for something they can believe in, something that offers security as well as a sense of focus. However, if we asked them to identify this need, it would be difficult for youth to articulate this desire in relationship to their faith. It is important for them to begin to grasp that church is not merely a Sunday place to talk about God and how lives were changed so many years ago. Church is a caring community where you can discover how your own life can be transformed when your faith is integrated into the everyday places of your life.

In a society that projects the "quick fix" image at every turn, it is vital that young people begin to explore the concept that faith is not a one-time destination or achievement, but rather is an ongoing relationship that has the capacity to grow throughout the rest of their lives. The activities in this session offer ways to supply some concrete images to the abstract concept of faith, and some opportunities for reflection that will enable youth to visually see how God has been present in their lives at all times—even if they did not recognize God's presence.

Scriptural Background

Scriptural Background
Scriptural Background

In Paul's letter to the Romans, he is striving to map out for them a pattern for living. The twelfth chapter is full of challenges for living a faith filled life. Paul realized that it is difficult to be "in" the world and not be "of" the world.

Rome was a powerful city—both politically and economically. It was the "heart" of the known world. Paul knew if the church of Rome could live out their faith that the world would be changed forever. It was a tremendous challenge that involved an incredible amount of risk, but the results would be phenomenal.

Teacher Suggestions

Read Romans 1:1 as you prepare to teach this lesson. Imagine what it would have been like to be a part of the church in Rome during the time of Paul. Was it more difficult to live out faith in Paul's day or today?

Review all the activities suggested for this week as you prepare to invite youth to explore their own faith journey. Remember that members of the group, including you, are at different stages of faith development and that we can learn much from hearing one another's story.

P•R•A•Y•E•R:

Dear God,

Open my eyes to see you in a new way today. As I share my faith with these young people, help us to see how you make the ordinary, extraordinary. Help me remember that we are all on the journey together and that I do not have to have all the answers. Guide us in paths that will show us your presence in our lives and in our hearts. Amen.

FAITH MAP

Mark significant events in life as well as times when you felt close to God—both highs and lows. (Examples: First day of school, death of a pet, birth of a brother or sister.)